Praise for *Of Course in Miracles*

Of Course in Miracles is a testament to Alan Cohen's unrivaled prowess as a storyteller, weaving together profound wisdom with the ease of a seasoned weaver at the loom of human experience. Alan once again demonstrates his gift for distilling complex spiritual principles into accessible, engaging narratives.

This book is not just a read; it's a transformative experience that challenges the reader to see the world not as a place of discord but as a classroom for peace. Cohen masterfully uses his own life's stories to elucidate the teachings of *A Course in Miracles*, making the book a personal journey as much as a universal guide.

Alan Cohen is the maestro of spiritual narrative, and his book is a symphony of wisdom that resonates with the soul's longing for peace and understanding.

— Bill Free
Spiritual Teacher and Executive Producer,
Awakening Mind Films

Of Course in Miracles is an excellent uplifting opportunity to more clearly understand how to truly live ACIM. Each chapter is as restorative as having a delicious coffee date with a wise and dear friend. It will make you smile, laugh out loud, and maybe even let go of some long held grievances. Alan's genius is that his stories stick with you and give clear inspiration for living a life of love. A perfect gift to anyone interested in *A Course in Miracles*.

— Jennifer Hadley
Founder, Power of Love Ministry

This book carries the amazing balance of being grounded and uplifting. The stories are personal, relatable, and inspiring. There is so much support and acceptance, from acknowledging how loved we are, to how we can always hear God, to the recognition that we don't have to struggle to try to belong in a world that does not resonate with our true self. *Of Course in Miracles* gives you the ACIM basics in a digestible, enjoyable, and healing way.

— Mark Anthony Lord
Spiritual Healer, ACIM Teacher and Student

After dealing with anxiety for many years, *A Course in Miracles* helped me find my way to higher ground. I very much appreciate Alan Cohen's expression of ACIM principles through his real-life examples, his humor, and his relatable stories and insights. *Of Course in Miracles* will help you apply ACIM to anxiety, fear, guilt, or any form of distress. I highly recommended this book for anyone wishing to get out of a rut and get your life moving in a positive, healing direction!

— Corinne Zupko, Ed.S.
Bestselling and award-winning author
of *From Anxiety To Love*

Super inspiring! A fun read about mastery and transformation that can change your life! Here is a bright reminder that we don't need to get to a place of power—"All the power you need is right within you, in the very place you stand, as you." Through Alan's gift of storytelling and personal examples, he shows us by his own demonstration how practical miracles are—how easy it is to look past appearances (problems, difficulties, body ailments)—and see and relate to ourselves and each other as souls. This book is for anyone interested in being established in peace, a how-to guide to stay in the quiet center even when there is chaos or conflict in the world or in your life.

— Lisa Natoli
Founder of The Healing Cure

Alan Cohen's voice for miracles is a true inspiration to me and to many ACIM students who wish to make the amazing benefits of the Course real in their daily life. *Of Course in Miracles* is an extraordinarily easy, gentle, and fun way to heal the mind and heart. I am touched by the depth and practicality of these shining insights. If you could use some miracles, this book will help pave your way!

— Maria Felipe
ACIM Teacher, Best-selling author of *Live Your Happy*

Alan Cohen proves to be a wonderfully skilled guide through the teachings of ACIM. *Of Course In Miracles* will provide both the new and experienced ACIM student with powerful insights and motivation to walk the ACIM path with their whole heart and make love their way of life.

— Aaron Abke
Author and Spiritual Teacher

By the end of *Of Course in Miracles* you'll be able to tune out the ego's frequency of fear and tune into the Holy Spirit's frequency of love.

— Matt McCabe
Co-Host of *Miracle Voices*

Also by Alan Cohen

Are You as Happy as Your Dog?
Baby It's You
A Course in Miracles Made Easy
A Daily Dose of Sanity
Dare to Be Yourself
A Deep Breath of Life
Don't Get Lucky, Get Smart
The Dragon Doesn't Live Here Anymore
Enough Already
Friends in High Places
The Grace Factor
Handle with Prayer
Happily Even After
Have You Hugged a Monster Today?
How Good Can It Get?
I Had It All the Time
Joy Is My Compass
Lifestyles of the Rich in Spirit
Linden's Last Life
Looking In for Number One
The Master Keys of Healing
My Father's Voice
The Mystical Messiah
The Peace That You Seek
Relax into Wealth
Rising in Love
Setting the Seen
Soul and Destiny
Spirit Means Business
The Tao Made Easy
Why Your Life Sucks and What You Can Do about It
Wisdom of the Heart

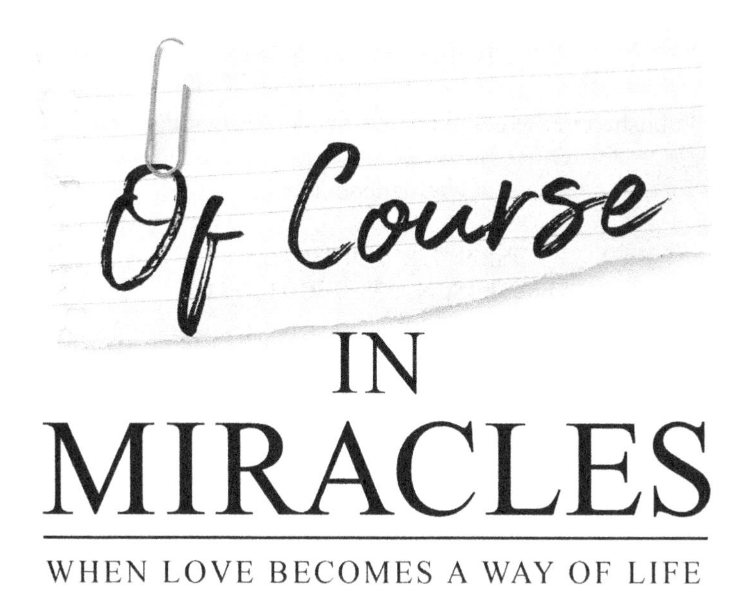

Of Course IN MIRACLES

WHEN LOVE BECOMES A WAY OF LIFE

ALAN COHEN

Of Course in Miracles: When Love Becomes a Way of Life

Published in the United States by Alan Cohen Publications
Post Office Box 662071, Lihue, Hawaii, 96766
www.alancohen.com

ISBN: 978-0-910367-28-8
Ebook ISBN: 978-0-910367-21-1

The author of this book does not dispense medical advice or prescribe the use of any technique as a form of treatment for physical, emotional, or medical problems without the advice of a physician, either directly or indirectly. The intent of the author is only to offer information of a general nature to help you in your quest for emotional and spiritual well-being. In the event you use any of the information in this book for yourself, the author and the publisher assume no responsibility for your actions.

All quotes from *A Course in Miracles*© are from the Third Edition, published in 2007 by the Foundation for Inner Peace, P.O. Box 598, Mill Valley, CA 94942-0598. www.acim.org and info@acim.org.

Cover design: Elena Karoumpali
Interior design: Isabel Robalo

Printed in the United States of America

For Helen, Bill, Ken, Judy
and all the Teachers of God
who have brought
A Course in Miracles
to humanity

Introduction

There is nothing quite like *A Course in Miracles*. I consider it a love letter from God to humanity. Its sweeping vision is grounded with practical exercises to relieve suffering and create enduring healing. The Course's wisdom, depth, heart, poetry, and capacity to transform lives are unparalleled. It contains all the truth that any individual, or humanity as whole, needs to be released from all fear, sorrow, and loneliness. Some of its lessons promise that if you master today's principle, you can save a thousand years groping about in a forest of painful illusions. ACIM is the ultimate "get out of jail free" card to escape the karmic wheel.

Several years ago I received an invitation from Ian Patrick, publisher of the online magazine *Miracle Worker,* to write an article for that publication, which showcases the teachings of the Course. It has been my honor to contribute an article for nearly all of the magazine's issues since that time, now under publisher Dan Strodl. Recently it occurred to me that these articles comprise a significant body of work worth sharing. That body comes to life in the book you are holding.

If you are not familiar with ACIM, a brief history is in order. The Course came as channeled material through psychologist Dr. Helen Schucman, and was subsequently recorded with help by her colleague Dr. Bill Thetford. The voice that dictated identifies itself as Jesus Christ. If there was ever proof that Christ lives, loves us, and walks with us, it is *A Course in Miracles.* The Course is an updated iteration of the teachings initiated by the Nazarene twenty centuries ago, clarified and packaged in language we can understand in modern terms. Rather than going into the Course's philosophy here, I will leave that for the chapters that follow.

This work is a natural progression from my earlier book, *A Course in Miracles Made Easy*. I am humbly grateful that many readers have found that book to be a helpful tool to understand the Course, which can seem abstruse and esoteric until we recognize its simple themes and universal applications. *Of Course in Miracles* provides fresh perspectives on ACIM, including a wealth of new stories that illustrate how to use the program for awakening and healing in all aspects of our daily life.

Although I have been working with this material for over forty years, I often feel like a beginner. There is no end to the depth and scope of the Course. I often laugh when I read in the Workbook introduction that the program takes one year. Many dedicated students continue to study and practice ACIM for a lifetime, gaining greater freedom, aliveness, and healing with each pass. If this book can contribute to you attaining those noble goals, whether you study briefly or for decades, it has served its purpose well.

Whether you are new to the Course, or you have been practicing for years, or you don't intend to study the program, but you wish to gain an understanding of its principles, you will find plenty of material here to get you started or take you to your next level. Truth has a brilliant way of finding you right where you stand, taking your hand, and guiding you to what will help you most.

The title *Of Course in Miracles* is an affirmation that miracles are natural. Workbook Lesson 77 calls us to remember, "I am entitled to miracles." The Course reminds us many times that a miracle is not an exception to the natural order of the universe; it is the *fulfillment* of the natural order. Some religions teach that miracles were reserved for the time of the Bible, but they are not available today. This is just another trick of the sleeping mind to keep love at a distance. Miracles happen every day, actually all the time. We just don't keep our eyes open to recognize them. ACIM corrects our vision so we see life clearly through the lens of love rather than the distorted view conjured by fear.

This writing represents my best understanding of the Course. I do not claim to be an infallible authority on *A Course in Miracles.* No person is, except the One who authored it. If any of my ideas do not accurately represent ACIM, please accept my apologies. I remain a student of the Course, continuing to learn as I go. Yet you should find enough guidance here to satisfy your hunger for truth and sustain you for a substantial portion of your journey. The Holy Spirit will reveal to you all you need to know through all the proper channels.

I am now entering into a dynamic teaching and learning relationship with you. As you absorb these ideas and elevate your life, you contribute to the upliftment of all humanity. Workbook Lesson 137 reminds us, "When I am healed I am not healed alone." Every time you experience an aha! moment through *A Course in Miracles*, the world becomes brighter, beginning with your own. Your awakening is your contribution to the healing of humanity.

Thank you for sharing this sacred journey. We are all going home together.

> Now you walk with Him, as certain as is He of where you go; as sure as He of how you should proceed; as confident as He is of the goal, and of your safe arrival in the end.
>
> —W-ep.4:6

Let us now hasten to the heaven we carry within us. Love calls us to claim our rightful place in the cosmos.

A Course in Miracles

A Course in Miracles is a self-study program of spiritual guidance comprised of three books: a *Text*, a *Workbook for Students*, and a *Manual for Teachers*. While all three elements are important, the key to mastering the Course is to practice the Workbook lessons. Staying with them faithfully, even if you do not understand all the lessons or you miss some of the practice periods, will help you gain the deepest benefits to transform your life.

While there are a number of different editions of the Course, the one I refer to in this book is published by the Foundation for Inner Peace, the original publisher of *A Course in Miracles*. The Foundation continues to work to translate ACIM into as many foreign languages as possible, 27 to date. The Foundation for Inner Peace offers ongoing free webinars, and has produced a handy app to help students master the program. You can read and search a free version of the Course at www.acim.org. The Foundation is a 501(c)(3) certified nonprofit organization, worthy of your financial support, and mine.

In this book I reference quotations from *A Course in Miracles* with the numbering system assigned by the Foundation. T stands for Text, W for Workbook for Students, M for Manual for Teachers, and S for Song of Prayer (an ancillary pamphlet). T-18.VII.5:1-3, for example, refers to Text, Chapter 18, Section 7, Paragraph 5, Sentences 1-3.

You can find my book *A Course in Miracles Made Easy* on Amazon.com in print and e-book format, along with an audio version in my voice. I have produced a video course accompanying that book, available via my website www.alancohen.com. I have also posted a series of 22 free YouTube videos, each illuminating one chapter of the book, available at @AlanCohenAuthor.

Contents

1

The Raisin and the Roach

"Oh my God—a cockroach!" Susan shrieked. I bolted off her couch, jarred by her cry as if a ten-foot cockroach was standing at her kitchen door. Instead, she pointed under the couch. Fearlessly I moved in that direction. (Growing up in New Jersey, cockroaches were some of my closest neighbors; I was on a first-name basis with many of them.) Susan followed close behind me. We both leaned over to inspect.

"It's not moving—it might be dead," she said, relief in her voice.

I picked up the creature and studied it. "You don't have to worry about this cockroach," I told her. "It's a raisin."

After we both had a good laugh, it occurred to me that Susan had lost her peace as much for a raisin as she would have for a cockroach. Physiologists tell us that when we get upset, a slew of toxic chemicals spews into our body that shortens our lifespan—or at least diminishes its quality. While

> When I am upset, it is always because I have replaced reality with illusions I made up.
>
> —W-52.I:5

getting bent out of shape over a raisin sounds silly, it's the story of all of our disturbances.

Yogis tell of a man who went to visit his friend in the country. During the night, the guest woke up to go outside to fetch some water from a well. Along the way, he saw a huge deadly snake coiled on the ground, poised to strike him. In the morning the host stepped outside and found his guest on the ground, dead. Beside him was a thick coiled rope, which in the dark the guest had mistaken for a snake. The man died of fright. Yet he was just as dead as if a snake had bit him. "The thoughts you hold are mighty, and illusions are as strong in their effects as is the truth." (W-132.1:4)

How much do we really need to be afraid? *A Course in Miracles* tells us, "Fear is not justified in any form." (W-240) The world is a big scary story we have made up. The fact that lots of people agree to the scary story does not make it true. We can withdraw our agreement in fear and reinvest it in faith. All worthy spiritual practices guide us to that crucial shift. "I could see peace instead of this." (W-34)

Every day presents a series of opportunities for us to choose peace instead of this. Our deepest purpose is to release ourselves, each other, and the world from the judgments that keep us in pain. When I was teaching in Japan, one of my students asked to interview me for his YouTube channel, and we made an appointment to meet at the end of the day. After my work day I went out for a bite to eat, and I forgot about our appointment. When I returned to my hotel room, he was patiently waiting for me in the hallway. I felt terrible about standing him up, and I apologized profusely. He graciously told me, "No problem."

At the end of our interview, he discovered there was an error with the camera setting, and we would have to repeat the interview. He felt bad about taking more of my time, but I told him, "No problem." We both laughed because we had taken turns forgiving each other.

A Course in Miracles would consider that session an ideal interaction because we both used it to release each other and ourselves from the burden of our judgments. From a human point of view, the interaction was flawed because we both made mistakes. From a divine point of view, the interaction was perfect because we forgave the mistakes. The Course would describe this meeting as one of "a series of holy encounters in which brothers meet to bless each other and to receive the peace of God." (P-2.I.4:1)

We all believe that someone or something has robbed us of peace. People do lots of cruel and foolish things. Neighbors gossip, a less qualified co-worker gets the promotion you deserve, and relatives misuse the money you gave them in good faith. There is no shortage of situations that seem unfair. Yet while we cannot control what other people do, we can choose our response. This is where our true power lives.

> I can be hurt by nothing but my thoughts.
>
> —W-281.I:5

The ego, or voice for illusion, has invented endless "causes" of our experience. Astrological configurations, number sequences, the economy, the government, food, weather, heredity, childhood traumas, viruses, pollution, incompetent workers, spouses who don't listen, and the aunt who still pinches your cheek at age 35, are but the beginning of a very long list of forces to which we seem to be vulnerable. Something "out there" is doing it to you or for you. But, the Course assures us, not one of these *apparent* causes has any power over our lives. We but do it to ourselves.

For this reason we must be extremely vigilant about the thoughts we focus on. "There *are* no idle thoughts." (T-2.VI.9:13) "What gives rise to the perception of a whole world can hardly be called idle." (W-16-2:2) You don't need a psychic to tell you what is going to happen. Tomorrow is today's thoughts grown up. Management consultant Peter Drucker wisely stated, "The best way to predict the future is to create it."

One of ACIM's key teachings is the reversal of cause and effect. The ego purports that the world is cause and our mind is the effect. This notion, like the entire world the ego has spun, turns truth inside out. Mind is cause and the world is effect. The world is but a mirror of our mind. The outside proceeds from the inside. To recognize that the world is a story we made up is the beginning of liberation from false causation and all the sorrow it engenders.

I once traveled with a group to visit the spiritual power places of Europe. This trip coincided with a time when a number of psychics and channelers were predicting that the world would come to an end. While our group was flying over France, an eight-year-old girl became fearful about the doomsday prophecies. She came to the group leader and asked, "Can we fly to a power place so we will be safe?"

The group leader smiled, put her arm around the girl, and told her, "We don't need to get to a power place, darling. *You* are the power place. All the power you need lives right where you stand, in you, as you."

We could all use that advice, especially when the world is embroiled in fear and we are tempted to battle external sources to wrest well-being from the clutches of evil. Many people believe this is the worst of times; humanity has fallen to the depths of depravity, and God is punishing the world for our sins. This is yet another ploy of ego. Nearly every generation has thought it was living in the worst of times; indeed there have been epochs on the planet far more dire than the one we face. I do not mean to minimize our issues, but to hold them in a broader perspective. During all apparent worst of times, there are those who have chosen to experience the best of times. They mobilized the power of mind to establish themselves in wholeness, grace, and higher vision, and extended kindness rather than succumb to divisiveness. They chose to bring heaven to Earth rather than sustain the conflicts that make Earth a hell. They reach out, join, and serve instead of retreating to fearful self-protection. Rather than depending on hand sanitizer to feel safe, they mobilize mind sanitizer. *A Course in Miracles* is the great purifier, purging our thoughts of vulnerability and replacing them with eternal safety.

> You are severely tempted to abandon Him at the outside ring of fear, but He would lead you safely through and far beyond.
>
> —T-18.IX.3:9

Take a moment now to consider the "roaches" in your life; all the things that seem scary; the people and events you must avoid or get rid of; the intruders that can invade or upend your well-being. What if they were all raisins masquerading as roaches? And even if they are roaches, so what? You are bigger than any roach. God did not say, "Behold, you are my beloved child to whom I have given command of heaven and earth. Except for roaches." You can decommission every fear by withdrawing the power you have attributed to it.

While some people call this the age of endarkenment, it is really the age of empowerment. The world ceases to be a battleground, and becomes a training ground for spiritual mastery. If you are studying *A Course in Miracles* or any worthy training, you are enrolled as a spiritual Samurai—not to do battle with others, but to join with them to defeat illusions by wielding the sword of truth. Then God Himself shall wipe away all tears, and no cockroach will be able to disturb the Son of God, which is you.

> He is as safe from pain as God Himself,
> Who watches over him in everything.
>
> –T-13.VII.7:2-3

Miraculous Insights:

1. What "roach" in your life is troubling you?
2. What does the voice of fear say to you about this person or situation?
3. What does the voice of love, trust, or confidence say?
4. How would you be thinking, feeling, and acting differently if you knew that you are in charge of your life, rather than another person, event, or cause?

Affirm:

I am in charge of my experience.

No person or thing
outside me can hurt me.

The power I seek lives within me.

I know the truth about myself
and my life, and I am free.

2

Where Heaven Kisses Earth

Just out of college, I volunteered to teach yoga in a veteran's hospital. I had no idea what I was getting into. There I found all the patients in wheelchairs, many with speech and motor impairments. Some were amputees. Their diapers smelled. Some just sat outside their room in the hallway all day long with no visitors. The facility was understaffed and overworked. Doctors and nurses were deflated and irritable.

I had never seen such suffering. I felt like Prince Siddhartha, who had grown up in a royal palace, sheltered from the ills that plague humanity. When Siddhartha ventured out beyond the palace wall, he encountered sick, old, and dying people. This stunning wake-up call moved him to try to understand how to escape the suffering of the world. Eventually he became the Buddha.

I was so distraught by my experience that the third week I was supposed to teach, I literally forgot to go. At that point I realized that if I was going to keep teaching at the hospital, I would have to find some way to be with these people and not get depressed.

I decided I would go back to the facility and focus not on the patients' bodies, but instead relate to their souls. I would not see them as broken and decrepit, but instead whole and empowered. Rather than fretting about their ills, I would have fun with them. During the next class, I guided the patients in a visualization in which I asked them to see themselves as 19 years old, running on a beach. A voice in my head chided me, "This is really cruel." But another voice said, "Just do as Spirit has instructed you."

The patients loved the class and the visualization. Many radiated bright smiles, tears of joy running down their cheeks as they surpassed their bodies' physical barriers and once again felt strong, healthy, and free. The patients thanked me profusely for the gift of this experience, and the following week they brought their friends. Eventually that class became the most popular in the hospital. Patients were lined up in their wheelchairs far down the hall, waiting to get in. The image reminded me of the final scene in the movie *Field of Dreams*, where thousands of cars were lined up to visit the baseball field where the physical world made a bridge to the spiritual.

> How lovely is the world whose purpose is forgiveness of God's Son! How free from fear, how filled with blessing and with happiness!
>
> —T-29.VI.6:1-2

The ego and Christ look upon two entirely different worlds. The ego sees bodies, while Christ sees Spirit. "And in Christ's vision He would show you the perfect purity that is forever within God's Son." (T-13.X.10:11). Transformed by such holy sight, a world of despair turns to one of hope.

A Course in Miracles guides us to bring healing miracles to a suffering world; to deliver kindness that releases us from the shackles of fear and judgment. Grace begins with higher vision, and leads to compassionate action. "God offers only mercy. Your words should reflect only mercy, because that is what you have received and that is what you should give." (T-3.VI.6:1-2)

Jesus underscores that *A Course in Miracles* works in everyday life. "This is not a course in the play of ideas, but in their practical application." (T-11.VIII.5:3) He does not shy away from earthly events that make the world seem scary. He calls us to look directly at frightening situations so we can see through and past them. In Workbook Lesson 14, Jesus cites the examples of war, cancer, heart attacks, and airplane crashes, thoughts that tend to make us cringe. Jesus mentions them so we can release them by recognizing that "God did not create a meaningless world." (W-14.6:8) He is using the events of the ego's world to lead us beyond that world to the real world.

In graduate school I served as Assistant to the Dean of Students. My first assignment was to respond to companies requesting recommendations for graduates who had applied for jobs. In most cases this was an easy task, as the students had done well in their studies and I could recommend them with confidence.

Then I received a request for a student who had done quite poorly in college. He had gotten bad grades, flunked out, and then returned. His record showed that he was anti-social, he had gotten into fights, and he had been placed on probation. He barely made it through college to graduate. In my opinion, he did not at all deserve a recommendation.

When I showed my proposed rejection response to Dean Blanton, he paged through the student's file and smiled softly. "Let's just write him a recommendation," he said. "We'll give the guy a chance."

As I re-drafted my response, I realized I had been given a teaching that far surpassed the psychology classes I was studying in. Dean Blanton forgave the student his errors and replaced condemnation with mercy. He wanted to help the student more than penalize him. He wanted to be a vehicle for the student to experience a miracle. To this day, many years later, that interaction stands as one of my most important memories of my education.

Our daily activities offer a wealth of invitations for spiritual awakening. It is tempting to want to retreat from the world. I often fantasize about going off to a nature retreat, cave, or monastery, and escaping the insanity we call life. While getting away for a while can serve a purpose, in the bigger picture we are called to master life from *within* life. Learning to maintain inner peace in a war zone is a far greater achievement than staying peaceful amidst quiet conditions.

My friend Karren was living in Los Angeles when race riots broke out. Her section of town was sieged with violence and looting. On the phone, I asked her, "How are you doing?"

She replied, "I am established in peace."

Karren refused to be seduced by an apparent breach of well-being. Her consciousness of the presence of love was her contribution to that awful situation. It's easy to hold the light amidst the light. But a light that shines in the midst of darkness goes much farther.

While Jesus taught the highest metaphysics, he was also extremely grounded. He took care of people in bodies on

Earth. When Jesus learned that John the Baptist had been killed, he set off to a remote retreat to pray and meditate. But a large group of people—we are told five thousand—followed him. So much for his quiet time alone! After three days, he grew concerned that the people had no food. He asked his disciples to gather what food they could, which amounted to five loves of bread and two fish. The master took these items and prayed over them, giving thanks to God. Then he asked the disciples to distribute the food to the masses. Miraculously, the loaves and fish were multiplied so everyone was fed, and there was even food left over. "Love is the way I walk in gratitude." (W-195)

This miracle inspires us to take good care of ourselves and each other in the material plane. Jesus did not tell the masses, "It's all an illusion. Forget about your body." He had compassion for their physical hunger, and he satisfied it. It's easy to talk spirituality, and harder to live it. Compassion guides us to meet people where they live, and relieve their suffering in the way most meaningful to them. We must show ourselves the same kindness. Anything we can do to minimize anxiety and stress constitutes a miracle.

The Course tells us, "Each day should be devoted to miracles." (T-1.I.15:1) I know of a man who suffered from deep depression. After he eventually worked his way out of the funk, he recalled that the person who helped him most during that dark time was a friend who came to his house every afternoon and massaged his feet for fifteen minutes. They exchanged hardly a word. "Today I am redeemed, and born anew into a world of mercy and of care; of loving kindness and the peace of God." (W-306.1:4)

Life on the planet can be difficult. Yet we can make it easier by offering kindness. Voltaire stated, "Life is a desert, but we can transform our corner into a garden." ACIM shows us how to cultivate this garden. While the Course appears to be intellectual, it is far more experiential. It's a hands-on program. If you try to process it through the thinking mind, you won't get very far. Even while the Course's words engage the intellect, its energy speaks to your soul.

In the movie *Pleasantville*, everyone lives in a dull, drab, black-and-white world. "The world is nothing in itself." (W-132.4:1) Then a few people find their passion for life. They begin to glow with vibrant color, like the radiant flowers they look upon. The "little" acts of everyday life bring color to a lackluster existence. When you ask your neighbor how her son is doing in school, or you thank the postal desk clerk for taping your package more securely, or you wait patiently for the stray dog to cross the street, you are bringing the world closer to heaven. "And they will hear the bird begin to sing and see the stream begin to flow again, with hope reborn and energy restored to walk with lightened steps along the road that suddenly seems easy as they go." (W-109.7:3)

I once had to reschedule a massage appointment. When I later told the massage therapist I had to reschedule again, I felt guilty. "Not a problem," he told me. "If you need to reschedule again, just let me know." In that moment the therapist was living *A Course in Miracles*. He was teaching me that my perceived sin had no effect on him.

What has no effect does not exist, and to the Holy Spirit the effects of error are nonexistent.

—T-9.IV.5:5

I sometimes hear people say, "It is what it is." They speak these words this in the wake of disappointing events, such as when a business deal falls through, or participants don't show up for a program. In a way, it is so. The world is what it is. Yet heaven, which occupies a dimension far beyond the disappointing world, also is what it is. It is to this divine "what is" that *A Course in Miracles* points us.

Miracles create an overlap where heaven kisses Earth, where the hand of God reaches through a portal and transforms the mundane to become divine. I continued to teach yoga in the veteran's hospital for seven years, until I moved away from the area. During that time I developed some of the most meaningful relationships of my life with people that society wanted nothing to do with, but whose inner light shined like beacons in the night. What started out as one of the most difficult experiences of my life turned out to be one of the most rewarding. Like the stunned but determined Prince Siddhartha, I found a way to rise beyond the suffering world, and claim a more heavenly existence. I had no idea what I was getting into.

Miraculous Insights:

1. Do you become distraught when you observe other people in pain?
2. If so, what higher vision can you hold of that person or group that empowers them and you?
3. Who do you hold judgments against?
4. How might you choose an interpretation of that person that will free both of you?
5. How might you take better care of yourself by having compassion for yourself and doing kind things for yourself?
6. How might you contribute to the physical well-being of someone you care about?
7. What can you do to make earth more like heaven?

Affirm:

I help others by holding the highest vision of them.

As I release others from the burden of my judgments, I release myself.

I love myself enough to take good care of myself.

Each day I make earth a little more like heaven.

3

Bears Don't Bite Innocent Children

Master spiritual teacher Florence Scovel Shinn was walking through a toy store when she came upon a display featuring a huge mechanical bear with flaming eyes, showing its teeth, growling fiercely. At the bear's feet stood a little boy looking up at the beast, smiling.

"Aren't you afraid of the bear?" Ms. Shinn asked the child.

"Not really," he answered. "Bears don't bite good little boys."

This simple encounter captures the essence of *A Course in Miracles*. We attract attack, conflict, and disease only because we believe we deserve pain and sorrow. When we know we are innocent, there is no reason for God or the world to punish us. All the lessons of ACIM are directed to help us recognize our nature as divine beings who deserve only good. "You will no longer doubt that only good can come to you who are beloved of God . . ." (W-151.10:3)

People who know they are innocent and loveable do not expect evil to befall them. It is only when we believe that we are sinful that we wait for the other shoe to drop. *There is no other shoe*. God is not waiting in the wings to punish you. You can punish yourself, but at such a moment you are not the instrument of God. You have made up a story alien to the will of God, and stepped into it as if it were true, while it is not.

> The guiltless have no fear, for they are safe and recognize their safety.
>
> —W-98.3:1

The Course maps in detail the psychology behind guilt and punishment. The ego, founded in the mentality of warfare, believes it has attacked God. It actually has—in its own warped perception. Yet an all-powerful God is not susceptible to any form of attack. Being love and only love, God has no perception of conflict. God reinterprets attack as a call for love by someone in pain. But the ego, unaware of God's eternal wholeness, believes it has injured God. While this line of reasoning is insane, so is everything the ego believes, and we should not be surprised at its twisted logic.

Taking the warfare mentality to its next logical step, the ego expects to be counterattacked by God. Here we see how the ego projects a jungle mentality onto heaven. Bodies attack and fight each other. Any wild animal that is attacked will respond with the same viciousness it has been dealt. So the ego falsely attributes beastly behavior to God, Who knows nothing of survival of the fittest. "The so-called 'battle for survival' is only the ego's struggle to preserve itself, and its interpretation of its own beginning." (T-4.II.9:3) Jesus assures us that struggle and love are quite incompatible. In heaven everything thrives in love forever.

Here is where guilt is born. The ego, expecting God to lower the boom on it in response to its attack, now fears retaliation. So it enters into a kind of plea bargaining with the Creator. The ego says to God, "I'll save you the trouble of punishing me. I will punish myself." Behind this offer the ego secretly thinks, "I will punish myself less than God would punish me." This deal is meaningless and tragic because any punishment the ego metes out is entirely unnecessary. We can sum up this entire dynamic by defining guilt as "punishing yourself before God doesn't."

If you believe you deserve to be punished, or you are waiting for the other shoe to drop, remember the little boy unafraid of the big bear because he knew he was good. No matter what sins you believe you have committed, you are innocent in the eyes of God. Jesus continually demonstrated grace by telling people that their sins were forgiven. The rabbis and Pharisees were aghast at his pronouncements, railing, "No man has the power to forgive. Only God can forgive." But Jesus was simply affirming that, from God's perspective, these supposed sinners were already forgiven.

> God does not forgive because He never has condemned.
>
> —W-46.I:1

We do not offset sin by making it real and then pleading for forgiveness or paying a penance. We undo sin by recognizing it is a trick of the mind, and has no reality or effect. "There is no sin." (W-101) Only in the world of illusion does sin wield a mighty sword and generate repercussions. If you believe you are only a body, mortal, killable, and subject to the slings and arrows of outrageous fortune, sins are real and formidable. But if you know that you are a divine spiritual being, created in the image and likeness of a perfect God, eternal, deathless, and invulnerable, no sin by

> Your sinlessness is guaranteed by God.
>
> —W-93

anyone else—or yourself—can touch you. Only in the dream of the world can we attack and hurt each other. *A Course in Miracles* guides us to wake up from the dream of bodies and sins, and claim our identity as unharmable beings of light.

A woman was having a nightmare in which a hideous monster was chasing her. She ran faster and faster, struggling to evade the vicious beast. Finally she smelled his terrible odor and felt his hot breath on her neck. The monster grabbed her by the shoulders, threw her down to the ground, and pinned her beneath him. She looked up at his horrid face and screamed, "What are you going to do to me???!!!" The monster shrugged his shoulders and answered, "I don't know, lady—this is your dream."

All monsters are dream monsters, with no more reality than a movie dinosaur. The characters in our dream play out the script we have written, for better or worse. You can project a horror movie or a love story onto a blank movie screen. The beastly bullies, saintly souls, accusers, and forgivers are all products of your mind. You cannot change a movie by charging the movie screen and trying to make the images of the characters act differently. But if you insert a new film into the projector, the actors will play out a new movie. ACIM is the ultimate mind training that teaches us how to transform our nightmare into a happy dream, along with all the characters that populate it.

The Indian sage H. W. L. Poonja, affectionately known as "Papaji," was an exponent of Advaita Vedanta, or "non-dualism," which is in many ways identical to *A Course in Miracles*. Papaji has a video called *Nothing Really Happened*, the title of which captures a major tenet of ACIM. Only in the world of illusion did something happen. "Nothing real can be threatened. Nothing unreal exists." (T-in.2:2-3) It seems as if we are born, we go through bodily changes, some people love us and others betray us, we get sick, and we die. Meanwhile none of those events really happened. All characters and occurrences in the dream are the progeny of *maya*, illusion. In reality, we remain whole, eternal, invulnerable, and made of only love and light. When the nightmare and the happy dream end, we re-emerge into pure positive energy, and all that remains is our true God Self. "Your other life has continued without interruption, and has been and always will be totally unaffected by your attempts to dissociate it." (T-4.VI.1:7)

> [Your brother's] errors . . . can have no effect at all on the truth in you.
> –T-9.III.6:6

I was touring the island of Kauai with my friend Ken Honda, a brilliant author and spiritual teacher. We arrived at a glorious vista point affording a stunning view of a pristine beach, verdant mountains brimming with waterfalls, and lush farmland. Ken exclaimed, "Wow! If you lived here and you died and went to heaven, you wouldn't notice any difference."

While Ken was joking, there was profound wisdom behind his quip. If you live in a heavenly state of mind while in the world, death is not much of a transition at all. You simply shift from one splendid room to another in the same golden mansion. The happy dream is the earthly version of heaven. That state of mind must be attainable, since Jesus taught us to pray, "On earth as it is in heaven." If earth is simply a hellhole, or a karmic retribution, or a penal colony, as some philosophers portray it, heaven here would not be possible. But it is. "'Heaven and earth shall pass away' means that they will not continue to exist as separate states." (T-1.III.2:1)

The key to transforming earth into heaven is to know that we deserve it. The little boy knew he was protected from a fierce bear, and, likewise, angels' wings enfold us. Voltaire said, "God gave us the gift of life; it is up to us to give ourselves the gift of living well." If you believe you must sweat, struggle, and sacrifice for your good, you are refuting the gift allotted you. Nothing makes God happier than for you to be happy. Since you are God expressing Itself, your happiness *is* God's happiness.

My mentor gave an affirmation we can all use:

The power of God is within me.
The grace of God surrounds me.

A poignant passage in the Text agrees:

Spirit is in a state of grace forever.
Your reality is only spirit.
Therefore you are in a state of grace forever.

—T-1.III.5:4-6

Scary bears exist only in a dimension outside of grace. When you are in your right mind, nasty beasts are invisible to you, and you are invisible to them. No harm can befall a Child of God. Innocence is our protection, and, no matter what the world tells us, we remain perfect. Rather than taking extensive measure to protect yourself from the evils of the world, meditate on your original innocence until you know yourself to be childlike and pure. Then you will recognize any bears you encounter as mechanical props in the toy store called the world.

Miraculous Insights:

1. What do you believe you deserve to be punished for?
2. How do you believe you deserve to be punished?
3. How much do you feel guilty?
4. How would you be feeling and living differently if you knew that you are innocent and you deserve only good?
5. If your life is a movie you are producing, how would you rewrite the script so everything turns out in your favor?

Affirm:

I am innocent.

I do not deserve to be punished.

God has already dismissed
any case against me.

I am free and I give freedom.

4

Don't Look at My Shoes

My friend Bette took her feisty teenage daughter Lexi to an appointment in town. As the two sat in a waiting room, Lexi commented on her mother's bright, frisky footwear. "Mom, how could you wear such ugly shoes?"

Bette, an ACIM student, smiled and replied, "If you don't like my shoes, don't look at them."

This light-hearted conversation offers a key teaching: Whatever we look at, we get more of. Attention is intention. Fascination is fertilizer. The vision you use determines the world you live in. If you focus on what you don't like, you will get more of what you don't like. If you focus on what you prefer, more of that will come. Some call this dynamic the Law of Attraction. More fundamentally, it is the Law of Perception. The Law of Attraction implies that there are things outside you that you draw unto you. The Law of Perception emphasizes that everything out there is already in here, in the storehouse of

> I see all things as I would have them be.
>
> —W-312

your mind, and you activate in your experience what you focus on. You are not in the world. The world is in you.

Many people do not receive what they want because they constantly focus on what they don't want. Jesus explained this principle very simply:

> To everyone who has, more will be given, and he will have abundance; but from him who does not have, even what he has will be taken away.
>
> —Matthew 25:29

While this dynamic may sound unfair, it simply explains a scientific universal principle. People who appreciate find more and more to appreciate. People who complain find more and more to complain about. Appreciators and complainers rarely find themselves in the same conversation. Each behavior operates at a different frequency. The Laws of Attraction and Perception join people of like vibration. If you consider yourself an appreciative person, and you find yourself with complainers, look within to see if there is something you are complaining about subconsciously. The external complainers mirror your internal complaints. If you are complaining about complainers, you have your answer.

Miracles demonstrate that you are in your right mind. At any given moment you are either aligned with truth or with illusion. Truth is empowering, illusion debilitating. Illusion can give you a "rush" or a "high," so you feel momentarily stimulated, but, like any addiction, in

> Miracles are examples of right thinking, aligning your perceptions with truth as God created it.
>
> —T-1.I.36:1

the long run it hurts. Truth brings you healing and life. The metaphysical minister Reverend Ike used to say, "You can't lose with the stuff I use." Thinking with God, or love, is the only train of thought that will take you where you want to go. Fear-based thoughts will take you down a dark rabbit hole. "Only the creations of light are real. Everything else is your own nightmare, and does not exist." (T-1.I.24:4-3)

We find whatever we are looking for because our vision is attuned to our desired object. I heard a rousing concert by a Trinidad band playing steel drums. They performed a menu of vibrant tunes, including the Hallelujah Chorus. Afterward, the band leader explained how they acquired their instruments. "After World War II, Trinidad was littered with empty oil drums left over from the army that occupied the island. They were everywhere! Some folks discovered that when they beat the empty drum with a stick, it made a musical tone. Then they figured out that if they altered the drum slightly, they could produce a different tone. So now the old army drums are tuned to generate uplifting music."

> For sight can merely serve to offer us what we would have.
>
> —W-312.1:3

Where the ego sees an instrument of war, the Holy Spirit finds an instrument of healing. *A Course in Miracles* trains us to shift our vision from the ego's limited world to the Holy Spirit's expansive world. At every moment we are choosing which world we will occupy. "Perception is a choice of what you want yourself to be; the world you want to live in, and the state in which you think your mind will be content and satisfied." (T-25.I.3:1)

The ego and the Holy Spirit each constantly scan the world to find objects that satisfy them. "The messengers of fear are harshly ordered to seek out guilt, and cherish every scrap of evil and of sin that they can find, losing none of them on pain of death, and laying them respectfully before their lord and master." (T-19.IV-A.11:2) Meanwhile, "Love's messengers are gently sent, and return with messages of love and gentleness." (T-19.IV-A.11:1)

A lady in my town complained to the Director of Public Works about the installation of a speed bump on her street. She was upset because the construction crew painted the warning on the road, "Hump." She argued that the city should not use a sexual term to describe the traffic control device. Meanwhile, every day hundreds of people drove over the bump, saw the sign, and thought nothing of it. But the lady was immersed in some judgmental mindset about sexuality, so her ego seized on that neutral sign to make it a threat worth complaining about. Fortunately, the Director denied her request to change the sign, and motorists now continue to enjoy uninterrupted happy humping.

The same Law of Perception applies to how we view our body. When you focus on bodily flaws or ills, you find more of them. When you focus on your inherent spiritual perfection, you escape disease. In ACIM Jesus tells us, "I raised the dead by knowing that life is an eternal attribute of everything that the living God created." (T-4.IV.11:7) Before you can raise the dead or heal the sick in the physical dimension, you must raise and heal them in your mind. You cannot generate healing while holding thoughts of sickness. They each belong to a different dimension, and you must "Choose this day whom you will serve." (Joshua 24:15)

My friend Audrey told me that some of her friends are getting cosmetic surgery at great expense. "I figured out how to save the many thousands of dollars they are spending," she told me. "When I look in the mirror, I don't look closely." While Audrey was being funny, she was alluding to a very practical spiritual principle. When you focus on the details of what's wrong with your body, you will get overwhelmed and depressed. If you pull your vision back and gaze softly, you will not be aware of the flaws. Then take this exercise to the next level, and look into your eyes until you discover your utterly perfect, beautiful, divine self. I heard a spiritual teacher say, "You don't need a face lift. You need a faith lift."

The more inherent wholeness you find, the more natural wholeness will become to you. I met a man on Maui whose grandmother lived until age 117. She lived in a very remote section of the island that has hardly been touched by modern civilization. In all of her life, grandma never rode in a car, watched television, or went to a doctor. She was immersed in a world of innocence and natural well-being. You don't have to live in a remote jungle to achieve that glorious state. You can recognize it right where you stand. "The kingdom of heaven is within you." (Luke 17:21) The key to finding that kingdom is to focus on it. Then it will expand.

Nowhere is the Law of Perception more apparent than in our intimate relationships, especially with a spouse. At every moment you are choosing the perception of your partner that creates and colors your experience. You generally do not see your partner clearly for who he or she is. Instead, you are seeing *your version* of your partner, for better or worse. On some days you may think, "I am so lucky to be with such a wonderful person!" On other days, you think, "I must have been crazy to get together with this wacko!" Your partner has not changed between those days. Only your perception has. The good news is that you are in charge of your perception. At any moment you can choose a new perception that works better for both of you.

> In the holy instant, where the Great Rays replace the body in awareness, the recognition of relationships without limits is given you.
>
> –T-15.IX.3:1

If you saw your partner as he or she really is—and who *you* really are—you would see a being of radiant light. Only our divinity is true. All else is distortion and illusion. While you have been taught that the purpose of marriage is to find that ideal soulmate who checks off all the boxes of your physical, emotional, intellectual, financial, cultural, religious, and sexual requirements, the deeper purpose is for your partner to help you purify your perception so you see them and yourself—as a magnificent spiritual soul. ACIM tells us that you will be appalled when you realize that the true purpose of your relationship is a platform to heal your mind. Unfortunately, nearly every romantic book, song, and movie glorifies special love at the expense of holy love, ego need over spiritual vision. For that reason, you must be determined and steadfast to use your relationship for healing rather than becoming more deeply entrenched in the illusions and unrealistic expectations and demands that keep so many people in such terrible suffering.

You probably had no idea that "Don't look at my shoes" would lead to such deep and all-pervading truth! But every human interaction eventually leads to God if we know how to follow the bread crumbs. "All things are lessons God would have me learn." (W-193) The next time someone criticizes you, or you criticize someone or yourself, remember Bette's comment to her daughter. Then shift your vision to something more rewarding, or find a way to appreciate the shoes. Every moment is a choice between ugliness and thankfulness. And at every moment we can make a new choice.

> Now I would choose again, that I may see.
>
> —W-52.4:6

Miraculous Insights:

1. How do you cause yourself pain by focusing on things you don't like?
2. Where else could you focus that would bring you peace and empowerment?
3. In an intimate relationship, what does that person do that annoys you?
4. How might you find inner peace by choosing to see a different version of that person?
5. How is that person helping you to grow spiritually?
6. What situation do you believe is costing you?
7. How might you change your experience by focusing on the benefits?

Affirm:

The vision I use
determines my experience.

I create miracles by
focusing on blessings.

The universe loves me
and takes care of me.

I am grateful for all the
gifts in my life.

5

The Holy Man and the Prostitute

An Indian *sadhu* (holy man) discovered that a prostitute was living on his street. As the sadhu watched men entering and leaving the prostitute's house, he grew quite irritated. The sadhu sat across the street and placed a stone on the ground for each of her customers. Eventually the pile grew quite high.

Years passed, and the prostitute died. Not long afterward, so did the sadhu. As he sat at the gate of paradise waiting to be shown to his heavenly estate, the sadhu saw the prostitute in heaven stretched out on a cushy chaise lounge beside the swimming pool of a sprawling mansion. She was sipping a cool drink, eating grapes, and laughing with friends.

Moments later, the gatekeeper guided the sadhu to his new home. The sadhu was shocked to find a small, cold hut made of dark stones similar to those he had used to count the prostitute's sins. Outraged, the holy man asked, "Why did that prostitute get a stately mansion, and I get a dismal stone hut?"

The gatekeeper answered, "Although that woman had an illicit profession, she had a good heart. She was trying to support her small child by the only means she knew. She was kind and compassionate to the men who visited her, many of whom were in emotional pain. You, on the other hand, were steeped in judgment. She inherited the afterlife that matched the consciousness she held during her life, and so did you."

I take this story more as an indication of the experience we generate *during* life, rather than afterward. *A Course in Miracles* is far more concerned with attitude than behavior. The "why" of what we do is far more important than the "what." We create our own heaven or hell by the consciousness we hold. When we release others from the brunt of our judgment, we release ourselves.

When I was in graduate school, I had a traumatic run-in with a professor. At a residential seminar, he got drunk and criticized me for the way I was leading my group. I took offense and answered him sarcastically. He lunged to punch me, until some other teachers in the room restrained him. The experience left me emotionally scarred.

As years passed, I cringed every time I thought of the incident. Then I attended a Christmas gathering where someone read Jesus's advice in the New Testament: "Before you bring your gift to the altar, make peace with your brother. Then come back and give your gift." (Matthew 5:23-24) What's the use of worshipping God if you hold enmity in your heart?

I wrote the professor a letter telling him that I regretted the incident, and I apologized for my part in it. I told him that I would like to consider our friendship like a fine wine that took time to develop. As I was about to drop the letter in the mailbox, a chill of fear rippled through me. *What if he laughs at the letter and continues to think I am a jerk? What if he comes back and tries to punch me again? What if he doesn't respond at all?*

Yet I knew I had to send the letter. I could not withhold it in fear of his reaction. I dropped the letter in the mailbox, and as I walked away, I felt incredibly free. Years of stress about the memory dissipated instantly. I did what I had to do. I was in integrity with myself, God, and my brother.

The professor never responded to my letter, and I never saw him again. But the lesson ran deep: When I forgave him, I was released. He chose whatever reaction he did, and reaped its results. But I was free. Now I could bring my gift to the altar with a whole heart.

A Course in Miracles tells us that the fastest and most direct way to come to God is to heal our relationships. If we say, "I love God," but we don't love our brother, we don't really love God because we have overlooked God in our brother. "I love You, Father, and I love Your Son." (W 298)

In the Text section, "I Need Do Nothing" (T-18.VII), Jesus explains that while we may engage in long periods of meditation, contemplation, and fighting against sin, although these methods ultimately get results, they are tedious and time-consuming, and we can reach our goal more quickly and efficiently by healing our relationships.

> Your way will be different . . . A holy relationship is a means of saving time. One instant spent together with your brother restores the universe to both of you.
>
> —T-18.VII.5:1-3

The world's idea of forgiveness is that we let someone off the hook after they have hurt us. But it is really *ourself* we let off the hook by releasing our judgment of the other person and our identity as a victim. Dr. Wayne Dyer used to say, "Resentment is like swallowing a spoonful of poison and then waiting for the other person to die." Lack of forgiveness eats away at the person withholding love, and can lead to emotional and physical disease. At the very least, it undermines our inner peace, the most precious commodity of life.

I know a massage therapist who worked in a hospital. One day she was assigned to massage an elderly cancer patient who was told she had but a short time to live. During the massage, the patient revealed that she had not spoken to her sister since the two had fought twenty years earlier. The massage therapist used her coaching skills to help the patient express her feelings, and the woman decided she wanted to heal with her sister before she died.

A few weeks later, the therapist was passing by the patient's room, and she looked in. To her astonishment, the woman was up and dressed, putting on makeup. She looked infinitely more vital and healthy. "What happened to you?" asked the therapist.

The woman smiled and answered, "After you and I talked, I phoned my sister and we made amends. I released my anger toward her, and I immediately began to feel better. The next time they took me down for testing, the doctor found no trace of cancer in me. I am going home."

> Look on your brother, and behold in him the whole reversal of the laws that seem to rule this world. See in his freedom yours, for such it is.
>
> —T-24.VI.5:1-2

This dramatic example demonstrates that genuine forgiveness heals the person giving it. What the other person does with forgiveness is up to them; they can receive it or reject it. Our job is to heal our mind. "Forget not that the healing of God's Son is all the world is for." (T-24.VI.4:1) "For we ascend unto the Father together. . ." (T-11.VI.4:9)

Everything in the ego's world reinforces the beliefs that created it. So it is with the forgiven world. When we dote on our brothers' sins, we keep ourselves from heaven. When we bless others with the right to enter heaven, we gain the same right. "My sinless brother is my guide to peace. My sinful brother is my guide to pain. And which I choose to see I will behold." (W-351)

In the Text section "The Forgiven World," Jesus asks us,

> Can you imagine how beautiful those you forgive will look to you? In no fantasy have you ever seen anything so lovely. Nothing you see here, sleeping or waking, comes near to such loveliness. And nothing will you value like unto this, nor hold so dear. Nothing that you remember that made your heart sing with joy has ever brought you even a little part of the happiness this sight will bring you. For you will see the Son of God.
>
> —T-17.II.1:1-6

A Zen aphorism explains, "You have no idea of the weight you have been carrying until you let it go." The most oppressive weights are judgment, criticism, and grievance. To walk daily through a dense world of separation, living as if you are but a body and personality, requires an unbelievable amount of veiling, burdensome defense, and contraction—all of which deplete our life force until but an ember of our original light shines through the thicket. Releasing judgment yields the greatest liberation. We may celebrate our political and social freedoms, but freedom from fear and judgment is far greater.

A popular television commercial showed a group of people wandering around in a dark room. Then a light came on and they found the coffee they were looking for. A godlike voice boomed, "Greetings, pilgrim, your search is ended."

It's not coffee we have been searching for, but peace of mind. (Although Starbucks has successfully equated the two.) ACIM tells us the only way we will find healing is through forgiveness. It's not that God will punish us if we judge. We punish ourselves by clinging to upsets. People who mutilate themselves are considered mentally ill. Yet we all self-injure when we hold judgments. When we drop grievances, we return to our natural state of well-being. Fear and love form a revolving door we walk through many times a day.

The day will come when we will quit spinning through that painful cycle. That day could be today. "I will forgive all things today, that I may learn how to accept the truth in me, and come to recognize my sinlessness." (W-119.2:2) While the Course offers many prayers, the simplest one is, "Just help me have a happy day today."

> This the day I seek my present happiness, and look on nothing else except the thing I seek.
>
> —W-290.1:6

Like the prostitute, we all do things that others who misunderstand us may judge us for. We may also identify with the sadhu who holds judgments about others or ourselves. Yet there is more to that story than that parable reveals. No matter what hut of cold stones you have constructed for yourself or another person, you are free to dismantle it. We all have the capacity to grow beyond being a victim or a perpetrator, and build a new life. All dark stories end in the light. This is the hope we can cling to with assurance and faith.

> Let me, then, forgive the world,
> that it may be healed along with me
>
> —W-82.1:5

Miraculous Insights:

1. Who do you think should be living differently from the way they are living?
2. How might they be either living in accord with their values, or learning lessons that will help them?
3. How do you think you should be living differently?
4. How are you justified to simply be yourself, and to learn lessons that will help you?
5. What are you fighting against in yourself or others, that is weakening you to fight it?
6. How might you come to greater peace by dropping the fight?
7. Is there any relationship in which you have become estranged?
8. What might you do to heal that relationship, either with that person, or within yourself?

Affirm:

*I do not have to fix
or correct anyone.*

*I trust that everyone is on their
right path, as I am on mine.*

*As I free others to live their chosen
life, I free myself to live my life.*

*I heal broken relationships
with love.*

6

Just Visiting this Planet

Do you ever feel like a misfit? Do the activities that entertain most people seem boring or meaningless to you? Do you find the Earth to be a crazy place, and you wonder what you are doing here?

If so, I have good news: There is nothing wrong with you, and you are not alone. Your sense of not fitting in with the mainstream indicates that your intuition is working perfectly. You are not the problem. The world is. Normal is the enemy of natural.

I like to swim at a beach where the Parks Department has placed huge boulders as a border in the ocean to form a protected swimming area. At the shoreline the water is ankle-deep, and it grows gradually deeper toward the boulder barrier. Most of the visitors to the beach simply wade where the water is just a few feet deep, up to their waist. I prefer to swim farther out.

One day when I arrived home from the beach, Dee asked me, "How was your swim?"

I told her, "The shallow area was pretty crowded, but that didn't affect me. Hardly anyone was in the deep section."

Hearing myself say those words, I realized I was speaking a metaphor: Most people in the world stay in the shallows, and relatively few go deep. If you are competing for space and commodities where life is shallow, you will run into lots of traffic. If you are willing to go deeper, there is hardly anyone else around.

My mentor Hilda Charlton presented a similar analogy: "Think of the world as a huge pyramid. At the ground level there are lots of people. As you rise in consciousness, there are fewer and fewer people. The closer you get to the top, the less company you have."

Some of my coaching clients feel lonely because they don't have many people in their life with whom they can relate on a spiritual level. Their family, old friends, neighbors, and workmates are not interested in talking about higher consciousness, healing, or the metaphysical dynamics behind the events of life. Nor do they strive to live spiritual values. I remind these clients, "Many are called, but few are chosen." While some people cite Jesus's teaching to mean that God selects a special few, there is a deeper meaning: All are called, but few choose to listen.

If you find yourself outgrowing the people and activities that used to be rewarding for you, consider one more scenario: You are at a party in a room with people who are talking about subjects and engaging in activities you once found interesting. After a while you get bored, and you step out into the hallway, where you hear voices from another room down the hall. These people are having much more engaging conversations than the ones you are used to. You feel drawn to enter that room, but it is a distance away. So you begin to walk down the hall, and about halfway along the way you start to feel lost, as if you are in a state of limbo. You have left the old room behind, but you have not yet arrived at the new room. At this point two key actions will help you: (1) Trust that you are on your right path, headed in the right direction; and (2) Keep moving forward. Keep your mind firmly set on where you want to end up. Think, speak, feel, and act on the new values you hold dear. Then the Law of Attraction will speed your journey and draw to you all the right people and conditions to support your new life.

In the meantime during your daily life, carry on with your regular activities, but do your best to maintain your higher consciousness. Be more concerned with your state of mind than your material acts. Infuse everything you do with love, no matter where you are, or whom you are with. Go through the motions, do the dance, but do not be distracted by mundane issues. Keep your head in the clouds and your feet on the ground. While your body walks the earth, your spirit is founded in heaven. Teach by your being. Jesus advised us to be the light of the world from within the world. You don't have to leave your life to heal it. You *are* life. You cannot be otherwise.

You are always connected to guidance. You will hear as much as you are open to receive. "The Holy Spirit's Voice is as loud as your willingness to listen." (T-8.VIII.8:7) While I was riding on an airplane listening to an uplifting spiritual lecture on my phone, the in-flight movie came on. I was sitting in the front row of the cabin, with a video monitor directly on the wall in front of me. It was virtually impossible not to watch the film, a teenage romance. The mindless plot was easy to track even without me hearing the sound. As I listened to the lecture with the greater part of my attention, and casually noticed the film, I was being given a profound lesson in how to relate to the world. Be aware of the non-sensical movie, but keep your mind established in the higher lecture. Divine wisdom is whispering in your ear. Heed that voice, and the inane illusion will fade to the background and eventually disappear.

Hilda Charlton lived in a rough section of New York City, where she encountered all kinds of wayward characters. One night a glassy-eyed street guy bragged to Hilda, "I am Joe, the king!"

Hilda looked the man in the eye and told him with loving firmness, "I know a greater King." Her statement pierced the man's heart. He began to weep, fell to his knees, and kissed Hilda's hand.

Hilda spent a great deal of her time communing with angels, ascended masters, and invisible entities. She was awakened every night at 3 AM, and recorded the messages she was receiving from a divine source. She could navigate the heaven worlds better than anyone I have ever met. Yet when she left her apartment, she was as savvy and world-wise as anyone. She managed money diligently and sized up people in a flash. The world was not a problem for Hilda. This saintly soul had so much leverage from a higher plane that the physical dimension was like kindergarten to her. (www.hildacharlton.com)

Many people I know feel as if they are not from this planet. Actually, none of us are. The world is not our home. We are just visiting. Our true home is in Spirit. Even while we walk this foreign land, we remain connected to our Source. Our happiness and well-being depend on our staying united with Spirit. When we cease to identify with our body and worldly attributes, we remember our identity as spiritual beings, and we accept the blessings we deserve.

A true savior participates in the world he or she is saving. You cannot redeem the world from a distance. A football coach stands on the field beside the players and guides them at ground level. He can help his team because he has stood on the same soil and walked the same journey they are now enduring. As saviors of the world—the Workbook assures us that is who we are—we must join with the people we are helping. Jesus was compassionate enough to walk the Earth and then dictate *A Course in Miracles*. He could have just sat on his throne of glory at the right hand of God and scoffed, "Let those dummies figure it out." Instead, he stepped into illusion to dispel it with truth.

Our role is identical to his. We must don the appropriate costume to blend in with the locals. We must go to Earth schools, learn Earth languages, attend Earth social functions, and circulate Earth money. Then we know the terrain, and we are qualified to help. A firefighter wears his gear to put out the fire, but when he gets home he removes it. He has a life that far transcends the fires he extinguishes.

When I entered the spiritual path, I thought I had to separate myself from mundane activities. My concept of holiness set me apart from people I believed were beneath me. Then one Christmastime I joined members of a yoga class to go caroling in a hospital. The yoga teacher entered the rooms of some of the patients and had very earthy conversations with them. "Oh, sure, I know where you live in Perth Amboy. I used to do shots in Tony's Bar on Lawrie Street." The patients would light up to meet someone who knew the local haunts. My yoga teacher demonstrated that connecting with people where they stand is far more helpful than being aloof. He was not at all interested in Tony's Bar now, but the memory provided a bridge from heart to heart. The pub was transformed to a healing tool.

We achieve mastery not by running from the world, but by *repurposing* it. The world is a place where we use our bodies to communicate by giving and receiving love. Any other purpose we ascribe to form will distract us and leave us unfulfilled. When we use the world for a higher purpose, we simultaneously act on stage and applaud from the audience.

Many of us vacillate between being very involved in the world and then stepping back from it. We get intensely immersed in our job or relationship, and then we need space. This is a natural cycle. We act and then integrate; get lost, and then find ourselves. In the early stages of our spiritual journey, these polarities are more extreme, even dramatic. We get deeply engrossed and then we need to deeply retreat. As we advance on our spiritual path, those contrasts become more subtle. More and more, we integrate our activities and our spirituality. Eventually we do not see a difference between the two. We use our worldly life as a template upon which to practice awakening. The world ceases to be our enemy, and it becomes our friend and teacher.

In the *Star Trek* television episode, "Errand of Mercy," the crew of the Enterprise is called to defend the planet Organia from an impending invasion by the Klingons. When Captain Kirk and his team arrive on the planet, they find the Organians' society to be very primitive. The people wear simple togas, they have no technology, and they do not bear weapons. The Enterprise crew pleads with the Organians to defend themselves, but they calmly refuse. Fearing the

Klingons will decimate this naïve civilization, Kirk becomes exasperated.

When the Klingons arrive, the Enterprise has a dramatic standoff with them. War is imminent. Just as Mr. Sulu is about to press the button to fire photon torpedoes at the Klingon vessel, the instruments on his control panel become too hot to touch. So it goes on the Klingon ship as well. Both factions are immobilized.

Then the Organians reveal themselves to be advanced souls. While their civilization seemed naïve, they were extraordinarily sophisticated. Their simple civilization was all they needed to touch the physical plane lightly. After teaching the Enterprise and Klingon crews the lesson, the Organians reveal themselves to be beings of brilliant light, and they disappear into a field of shimmering energy. They were not their apparent bodies at all. Their physical world was a vehicle for their spirits to take momentary expression. They were in their world, but not of it.

We now stand on the same threshold that the Enterprise crew and Klingons experienced. While the world seems steeped in war, disease, and confusion, our true life runs far beyond physical appearances. Yet we can work the physical plane in favor of Spirit. Eventually our weapons will be too hot to handle, and we will be still an instant and go home.

Miraculous Insights:

1. Do you think you are weird, an outcast, or a misfit?
2. How has not fitting into the mainstream served you?
3. How might your uniqueness be a blessing and an asset to the world?
4. Where and with whom do you fit?
5. How can you cultivate relationships and participations that match your true self and unique intentions?
6. How might you and your life be perfect just as you are?

Affirm:

I am here to live my unique life
and deliver my unique gifts.

I fit in where I belong.

I have a community of souls who
match, love, and support me.

The universe rewards my courage
to live according to my values.

7

Miracles through Your Hands

A Course in Miracles regards every student of the Course as a miracle worker. You would think that such an eminent title would be reserved for Jesus Christ, Mother Teresa, ballplayers who score the winning point during the last second of a match, and middle school teachers. Yet Jesus himself calls you and me miracle workers.

Jesus's validation of our divine role began with his first words to Course scribe Dr. Helen Schucman. While most people believe that he initially dictated, "This is a course in miracles. Please take notes," Jesus made another statement to Helen before the Text began. He said, "I will work miracles through your hands."

Helen Schucman did not at all fit the profile of a miracle worker. She was a clinical psychologist trained in Freudian therapy, Jewish by culture, and agnostic by philosophy. She was often nervous, and embroiled in ongoing conflict with her boss. Helen intensely resisted receiving *A Course in Miracles*, and even after she surrendered she was highly reluctant to be associated with it. You would think that if

Jesus was recruiting a scribe for his world-changing tome, he would pick someone more, well, spiritual.

But the Helen Schucman who presented a particular personality to the world was not the Helen Schucman who had made a soul contract with Jesus Christ to deliver this cosmic testament to humanity. We can't judge by appearances. And since the whole world is an appearance, we can't judge at all.

Jesus's initial words to Helen were not just for her. They were for all of us. We are called to deliver miracles on a daily basis. We don't receive healing just for ourselves. We are required to pass healing along to others. "When I am healed I am not healed alone." (W-137)

Each day should be devoted to miracles.
—T-1.I.15:1

Sometimes we consciously work miracles, but more often they work through us in the course of daily life. If you receive an unexpected intuition or inspiration, you are likely participating in a miracle.

While I was delivering a lecture at a holistic health conference, I recounted a day when I went into a convenience store to buy some potato chips. When those words left my lips, I felt embarrassed. Potato chips are a no-no for holistic eaters, especially the kind of chips that come from a convenience store. I went on with my lecture, hoping the audience would forget my *faux-pas*.

After the lecture, a well-known healer approached me. I figured he came to criticize me. Instead, he smiled, shook my hand enthusiastically, and told me, "I just want to thank you for talking about potato chips. Sometimes I binge out on ice cream, and I feel guilty. When I heard you, a spiritual teacher

I respect, admit that you eat potato chips, I forgave myself. I am healed!"

Jesus said, "It is not I, but the Father within me who does the work." (John: 14:10) So it is for all of us. If you try to perform a miracle, you are likely doing the ego's bidding. But if you just show up and follow the voice of loving guidance, remarkable results accrue.

> Miracles are habits, and should be involuntary. They should not be under conscious control. Consciously selected miracles can be misguided.
>
> –T-I.I.5:1-3

At one time I was flying from New York to Hawaii, and I had to change planes in San Francisco. My first flight was delayed, and it arrived after the final flight of the day to Hawaii. The airline agent told me that I would have to find a hotel at my own expense, and take the first flight out the next morning.

Beside me at the agent's desk I noticed another fellow in the same predicament. He looked clean cut and respectable, so I asked him if he would like to share a room and save some expense. He thought for a moment and said, "Okay."

We went to the hotel, chatted for a bit, exchanged business cards, and retired for the night. I woke up early the next morning and caught my replacement flight. Meanwhile I wondered if inviting him to share the room was a rather forward and unnecessary move.

Ten years later I received an email from the fellow. He told me, "I have to admit that I had second thoughts after agreeing to share the room with you. I even slept with my wallet under my pillow."

He went on, "I saved your business card and checked out your website, where I found a list of your books. I am a counselor at a facility for young people who have gotten in trouble with the law, mostly for drug-related offenses. I purchased a copy of your book *Why Your Life Sucks and What You Can Do About It*, thinking it might help my program participants. It became a real hit! I have since given many copies as gifts to my clients, who are putting your ideas into action, and changing their lives. I just wanted you to know what became of our "chance" encounter, and thank you for making a huge contribution to uplifting the lives of people who can use lots of help."

> A miracle is never lost. It may touch many people you have not even met, and produce undreamed of changes in situations of which you are not even aware.
>
> –T-1.I.45:1-2

Little did I know that inviting that fellow to share a room would set in motion a series of miracles, the end of which I will never see. The flight delay, late arrival, and lack of a connecting flight were elements of a far greater design. Anytime you choose love over fear, you are setting a miracle, and probably many, in motion.

The world needs all the miracle workers it can get. Many people are steeped in fear, confusion, and despair, and need help. I meet lots of people who would like to put their writing, teaching, coaching, healing, art, or music out to the world, but they don't feel worthy or ready. Or they are shy to admit and express their spiritual beliefs and visions. I tell them that even if they help one person, their authentic self-expression is worth it. The voice of unworthiness is always ego. Jesus wouldn't have called us miracle workers if he didn't see something greater in us than we see in ourselves.

Move ahead even if you feel afraid, unworthy, or guilty. "The presence of fear is a sign that you are trusting in your own strength." (W-48.3:1) Spirit, the real miracle worker, is our true strength. The difference between people who accomplish great things, and those who don't, is that those who do great things step forward even while fear still pokes at them. They trust that more good than problems will come from their actions. ". . . Trust remains the bedrock of the teacher of God's whole thought system." (M-4.III.1:6)

> You are perfectly safe as long as you are completely unconcerned about your readiness, but maintain a consistent trust in mine.
>
> —T-2.V.4:2

While we believe we need God to help us perform miracles, which we do, God needs us just as much. We are the conduits through which miracles come to the world. Food does not usually magically materialize before a hungry person, or a house sprout from the earth to shelter a family in need. But caring people find ways to provide meals, and groups like Habitat for Humanity build homes as gifts. Such service is just as much a miracle as if the meal or house manifested out of nowhere. We participate in the miracle process in co-creation with God.

> You are my voice, my eyes, my feet, my hands through which I save the world.
>
> —W-rV.in.9:3

Workbook Lesson 156 urges us to ask a thousand times a day, "Who walks with me?" (W-156.8:1) I used to answer this question by naming the Holy Spirit, Jesus, God, and other invisible or angelic entities. Now I include living, breathing human beings as my valued divine companions. Countless people have helped me in tangible, practical, physical ways. Many caring souls have also been there for you, and made your life easier. God walks with you through your dear friends and those who have been kind to you at crucial crossroads. Love has abandoned no one.

After a man passed from the earthly dimension, a heavenly guide was giving him a tour of various rooms in the world to come. The guide opened a door where the man saw a group of people hovering around a huge banquet table filled with a lavish display of food. But the diners' tummies appeared to be empty and their faces were gaunt. As the man looked closer, he saw that everyone was holding spoons longer than their arms, so they could not get the food into their mouths. They were starving. "That, sir, is hell," the guide informed the visitor.

Saddened, the man asked, "Then please show me heaven."

The guide ushered the fellow through a corridor and opened another door. There he saw the same scenario he had observed in the previous room—a sumptuous feast with a large group surrounding the table, holding spoons longer than their arms. But in this scene, everyone's tummy was full, they were smiling, and they looked radiantly healthy. As the man studied this group more closely, he understood the difference between hell and heaven: The people in heaven had learned to feed each other.

Miraculous Insights:

1. What acts of love or kindness have you done that have uplifted or improved the lives of others?
2. What specific action is your intuition now guiding you to do to bring healing to the world?
3. Are you ready to accept your role as a miracle worker?
4. If so, what would be your next step to make your service real in expression?
5. Can you trust that as you offer yourself in service, the Holy Spirit will guide and work through you?

Affirm:

I am open and willing
to be a channel for miracles
to bless the world.

I gladly do whatever I can to relieve
suffering and uplift lives.

I trust and allow Spirit
to work through me.

I am always well guided, and I act
on my intuition successfully.

8

Bless the Cage Rattlers

Waking up in the country is peaceful and inspiring—until you enter your pantry and find that a rat invaded it overnight and left a huge mess. When one morning I found such a rude surprise, I bought a humane cage trap and set it that night. Sure enough, the next morning I found the marauder scurrying in the cage, and I took it out in a field to release it. But when I opened the door of the cage, the rat did not run out as I expected; instead, it clung to the back of the cage. I tilted the cage and shook it, but the stubborn critter did not move. Finally I gave it a good, strong shake, and the rat jumped out and scampered away to freedom.

We tend to be like the rat who clings to the cage rather than accepting freedom when it is offered. We find a twisted safety in bondage, and regard release as threatening. Thus people who "rattle our cage" are helping dislodge us from a fear-constructed trap. The question is, "How much shaking do

> Have you really considered how many opportunities you have had to gladden yourself, and how many of them you have refused?
>
> –T-4.IV.8:1

you need before you will exit the cage and march to freedom?" In his classic book *Illusions*, Richard Bach says, "Argue for your limitations and, sure enough, they're yours." Ultimately no limits belong to us, but we can clutch to them persistently until we identify with captivity rather than our innate freedom.

"The Bible tells us that a deep sleep fell upon Adam, and nowhere is there reference to his waking up." (T-2.I.3:6) We have all gone to sleep and we are dreaming the ego's world. We all need to awaken. Our life is a series of lessons to help dislodge us from illusion and reclaim reality.

We can wake up the easy way or the hard way. I used to have an alarm clock that blared like a fire engine. It was so loud and abrasive that I thought it would wake up the entire neighborhood. Then I discovered a Zen alarm clock that played a soft, sweet, melodic chime. The contrast between the Zen alarm and the bomb alarm was amazing. What a delight to wake up to a soothing, meditative tune rather than a psychic explosion!

We learn by contrast. When we make decisions contrary to the Holy Spirit's guidance, we head down a long, bumpy, painful, dead-end road. Then we have no choice but to turn around and go back to the crossroads where we gave in to the voice of fear, and make a new choice in favor of love. "Choose once again if you would take your place among the saviors of the world, or would remain in hell, and hold your brothers there." (T-31.VIII.1:5) In our human journey we toggle back and forth between darkness and light, until we choose in favor of Spirit.

How long that exploration takes, and how hard it gets, is up to us. If we are ornery and resistant, we will get banged around by the world until we are beaten and scarred and our life feels like a nightmare. The purpose of *A Course in Miracles* is to shorten, lighten, and ultimately relieve us of the nightmare and replace it with a happy dream.

> Tolerance for pain may be high, but it is not without limit. Eventually everyone begins to recognize, however dimly, that there *must* be a better way.
>
> —T-2.III.3:5-6

In the happy dream we still participate in the illusion of duality, but we use it for the Holy Spirit's purposes rather than the ego's. We still have relationships involving bodies, but our goal becomes joining rather than getting. We may still go to work, but our intention is to connect with our peers and clients and help them rather than amass money, compete, or build an egoic empire. We may still watch movies or television, but we seek to extract uplifting lessons rather than numb ourselves with mindless distractions. Thus we are constantly, gradually moving to higher ground, our path lighted with miracles. It is said, "When you take one step toward God, God takes ten steps toward you."

The voice of the Holy Spirit is always gentle and never screams or demands. You can be sure that any screaming or demanding is ego. The ego can, and often does, drown out the still, small voice. Then we get into some predicament that shows us we followed the wrong guide. When I studied with Hilda Charlton, a fellow student gave her a car and asked me to drive it to Hilda's evening class in Manhattan to deliver it. After the class I told her, "I have your car."

Hilda thought for a moment and replied, "How about if you bring it in next week?" Hilda had taught us that spiritual masters never give random or meaningless instructions. Their advice is always connected to Big Picture Guidance. But I wanted to be the one who delivered the car, and *tonight*.

"That's okay," I replied, "You can take it tonight."

Again she suggested I wait. This conversation went on for another round until she finally agreed to take the car that night.

Feeling triumphant, I went down into the subway to make my way home. Yet I was unfamiliar with the subway system and I took the wrong train. Twenty minutes later I stepped out of the train into a station in the South Bronx late at night. Looking around at some pretty rough characters, I regretted my decision to force the car on my teacher. I turned around and took the next train back without mishap. But I learned an important lesson in not attempting to override the voice of love with an egoic demand.

We've all taken the wrong subway, and, like the prodigal son, found ourselves starving in a foreign land. Eventually we realize that we've traded our Father's abundant estate for a cheap substitute. Then we turn about and begin to retrace our steps to peace. For some of us, that turning point needs to be dramatic to get our attention. We might experience a physical illness, a divorce, or a financial setback that rocks our world. But the rocking is not a punishment. It is a blessed course correction. "Free will does not mean that you can establish the curriculum." (T-in.1:4) "Only the time you take it is voluntary." (T-in.1:3) Sooner or later we all find our way home.

Ultimately, ACIM teaches, suffering is not required. We can achieve our goal fluently and joyfully. "When you have learned how to decide with God, all decisions become as easy and as right as breathing. There is no effort, and you will be led as gently as if you were being carried down a quiet path in summer." (T-14.IV.6:1-2). *A Course in Miracles* is the definitive answer to the question, "How easy can it get?"

When Jesus describes the crucifixion as "the last useless journey" (T-4.in.3.1), he is teaching that he didn't need to be crucified, and neither do we. This instruction flies in the face of fundamentalists who insist that crucifixion is a prerequisite to resurrection. In ACIM, Jesus instead underscores that we can wake up to a whisper rather than an earthquake. Like a loving parent, God calls to us kindly. God is not angry; that image is a projection of a human trait. Recognizing God as compassionate and forgiving is one of the key turning points on our spiritual path.

Meanwhile, a part of us clings to the known world as a source of safety, even though it is flimsy and unfulfilling and has continually failed us. One of my students reported, "Everything I have to let go of, I leave claw marks on." Yet Jesus comforts us, "Fear not that you will be abruptly lifted up and hurled into reality. Time is kind, and if you use it on behalf of reality, it will keep gentle pace with you in your transition." (T-16.VI.8:1-2) The Course is practical and works with us where we are, holding the vision of our full release even while we cavort in a far country.

In the film *Joe Versus the Volcano*, Meg Ryan's character issues a powerful teaching: "My father says that almost the whole world is asleep. Everybody you know. Everybody you see. Everybody you talk to. He says that only a few people are awake, and they live in a state of constant total amazement."

A Course in Miracles would have us be among those awake and amazed. Our Teacher would love for us to achieve liberation with grace and ease. The Holy Spirit is ever available to show us the path without pain, and to set our feet softly on higher ground. In the material world, we may sometimes feel like a trapped rat. Yet the cage has a door. No matter how long you have been trapped, you can exit in one golden moment, and scamper to freedom.

Miraculous Insights:

1. How might a person or situation that disturbs you actually be helping you?
2. How might a challenging situation you face be helping you get out of a rut?
3. What wake-up call might the benevolent universe be giving you?
4. What messages have you been taught, overtly or subtly, that claim you must suffer in order to please God or enter heaven?
5. Would you be willing to question or challenge those messages, and accept that your joy heals the world more than your suffering?

Affirm:

I appreciate challenges as
a venue for me to grow and
enjoy greater freedom.

I allow wake-up calls to
lead me to a better life.

I listen to whispers from
Spirit and I act on them.

My happiness is my gift
to the world.

9

A Higher Education

My neighbor Ron is a retired homicide detective. Nearly every day of his twenty-five-year career, he visited murder scenes in Los Angeles. I asked Ron, "What did you learn over such a long time in that position?" I braced myself, expecting some maudlin response.

Instead, Ron smiled and answered, "I met lots of really nice people."

I was shocked! This man was immersed in one of the grisliest jobs imaginable, and instead of remembering corpses and criminals, he recalled the valuable relationships he developed. Ron still wears a baseball cap with "homicide" printed on the front. To him, the memory is positive. (The full Irish bar in his basement helps stimulate his uplifting reframes.) As Shakespeare noted, "There is nothing either good or bad, but thinking makes it so."

Ron is what *A Course in Miracles* would call "a happy learner." He typifies the skill, "Take what you have and make what you want." ACIM consistently tells us that

> Projection makes perception, and you cannot see beyond it.
>
> —T-13.V.3:5

the world is a blank screen upon which we project our thoughts. Is being a homicide detective a horrible job or a rewarding one? That depends on the thoughts you apply to it.

Everything we think we see is in our mind. A serene sunset mirrors peaceful thoughts. Newscasts filled with violence spring from violent thoughts. A stunning starry sky expresses our belief in magnitude. A mean boss reflects self-judgments. While it seems that we live in a physical universe, we live more fundamentally in a universe of ideas. Some of our ideas empower us, and others hurt us. Daily we have many opportunities to transform hate mail into love letters.

After Dee and I moved into our new home, I applied for a post office box. When the postal agent assigned our box number, I didn't like it. I prefer certain numbers and combinations, and these numbers were not it. I thought about asking the agent for a different box, but then I realized that I had given my power away to numbers. I made them into magic, believing that certain numbers can help me and others can hurt me. Immediately a series of Workbook lessons streamed into my mind: "I am under no laws but God's." (W-76) "I am affected only by thoughts." (W-338) "I can elect to change all thoughts that hurt." (W-284) So I decided to keep the assigned box as an affirmation that I can be completely happy even with numbers my ego doesn't prefer. Now I like the box number because I receive loving letters and checks there.

> I am responsible for what I see.
> I choose the feelings I experience, and I decide
> upon the goal I would achieve.
> And everything that seems to happen to me
> I ask for, and receive as I have asked.
>
> —T-21.II.2:3-5

The ego does not want to hear the above affirmation of our creative power. Its entire world depends on being a victim of external forces, so it constantly projects our well-being onto objects, people, and places. Until we claim our innate wholeness, the world is a puppeteer pulling our strings. We run to and fro, hoping that the next savior will liberate us. We chase gurus, stand on Sedona vortexes, and sport protective jewelry. We are petrified to leave our house because Mercury is in retrograde. We fantasize about the perfect soulmate who will complete us. In many cases we find relief, but not because these items or people have the power to heal. We have chosen to be healed, and we use these objects as permission slips to attain our desired result. We needed none of them. We simply needed the power of God that we already own.

French homeopath Christian Almayrac is known as "Dr. Happiness." He presents one simple teaching: At any given moment, ask yourself, "Is the thought I am currently thinking the happiest thought I can think?" If not, "What is the happiest thought I can think instead?"

While this technique seems simple, it is quite profound and represents the heart of ACIM. The Course is far more interested in what we are thinking than what we are doing. The only thoughts that will make us happy are God's

> . . . All creation lies in the thoughts I think with God.
>
> –W-51.4:8

thoughts. The rest take us deeper into nowhere. The Apostle Paul urged, "Let the mind be in you, which was also in Christ Jesus." (Philippians 2:5)

While walking in a park, I saw a teenage boy toss an empty plastic soft drink bottle toward a trash can. He missed, but didn't bother to pick it up, and kept walking. Quickly my mind fell into judgment: "Lazy kid . . .Why don't parents teach their kids to respect the environment?" and on and on. As I got closer to the trash can, I saw that behind it, out of my view, was a recycling can, its rim at a lower height than the trash can. The boy had put the bottle in the recycling can. My judgments were unfounded. The time and energy I had invested in judgment were entirely wasted.

The park, like the world, had become my classroom, showing me how easy it is to be fooled by appearances. That boy was my teacher, sent by Holy Spirit, to facilitate my awakening. Even if he had tossed the bottle on the ground, judging against him would not make my life, or anyone's, any better. We think, "If I can get people to behave as I prefer, and rearrange my environment to please me, I will be happy." But we can never huff and puff enough to get the world lined up with all of our desires and expectations. Instead, we must recognize the presence of love. Then we can let the world be what it is. "What can frighten me, when I let all things be exactly as they are?" (W-268.1:6) Then we rest serene in the inner temple of peace, where the flame of truth cannot be disturbed by the winds of outer change.

All experiences come for one of two reasons: to be enjoyed or to be learned from. If we are not enjoying, we are learning. Any moment of upset, no matter how small, is a call to shift from our wrong mind to our right mind. "As the world I see arises from my thinking errors, so will the real world rise before my eyes as I let my errors be corrected." (W-54.1:5)

While many of us have striven to attain degrees in higher education, spiritual education plumbs to the core purpose of our earthly journey. We can learn all kind of facts and figures about how to navigate the material world, and still feel lost. Many people hide in the intellect and academia, and remain empty and lonely. Ram Dass's teacher Hari Dass Baba taught him, "Painted cakes do not satisfy hunger."

In college I was a psychology major. I performed well and graduated *magna cum laude* and *phi beta kappa*. I learned a lot about lab rats, statistics, and mentally ill people. But I did not learn how to live. I don't remember much of the course material. Many of my professors were not happy people or very healthy psychologically. They were embroiled in competition, argued regularly, and were depressed. Their academic tools worked behind ivy-covered walls, but when they went home they were forlorn. They modeled fragmentation more than wholeness. I remained hungry for truth.

In graduate school I found a humanistic psychology program that valued people more than rats. The teachers were authentic, strove to follow passion, and encouraged me to shine my inner light more than regurgitate answers on exams. I felt seen and loved. I experienced a 180-degree shift toward realness. That was the beginning of my spiritual path that led me out of the woods and into the sun.

Everyone is our teacher. Some teach us what to do, and others teach us what not to do. More specifically, some teach us how to think and others teach us how not to think. Certain thoughts we hold bring us closer to peace, and others distance us from peace. Eventually we learn which thoughts work and which don't work. While we may set out to conquer the world, our real task is to conquer our mind. Holy Spirit brilliantly sets up situations and draws to us people who help us learn the lessons tailored for our personal curriculum. Then we gain the master's degree that makes the entire adventure worthwhile. We are all guaranteed to graduate. Let us pray that day comes soon.

Someday, after mastering the winds,
the waves, the tides and gravity,
we shall harness for God the energies of love, and then,
for a second time in the history of the world,
man will have discovered fire.

— Pierre Teilhard de Chardin

Miraculous Insights:

1. How could you view a difficult situation from a new perspective that brings you relief or peace?

2. List three significant people or situations in your life that are joyful and/or challenging:

   1. ....
   2. ....
   3. ....

3. What thoughts that you are holding in your mind do these people or situations reflect?

   1. ....
   2. ....
   3. ....

4. What people or situations do you tend to imbue with undue power over you?

5. How would you relate to these people or situations if you took your power back from them?

6. What is the happiest thought you could think at this moment?

Affirm:

I am grateful for everyone and
everything that helps me
grow spiritually.

I choose the highest view
of all of my experiences.

As I practice right thinking,
all of life works in my favor.

10

Love Finds You Where You Are

In the classic film *Lost Horizon* (1937 version), statesman Robert Conway is kidnapped and taken to the fabled Shangri-La, tucked away in the remote Himalayas. There he discovers a utopian community where people live in harmony, everyone's needs are met, and love is the abiding reality.

Yet after a while doubts overtake Conway, and he becomes convinced that Shangri-La is fake. So he departs and returns to his worldly life. Then he realizes he has made a terrible mistake. Shangri-La is true, and the "real" world outside paradise is the illusion. He must then make a huge effort to find his way back.

Like Conway, we have all turned our back on paradise. Heaven is our home; nothing less will fulfill us. We have been in the presence of love all the while, but we were distracted, looking elsewhere. Now we must find our way back.

> Ours is simply the journey back to God Who is our home.
>
> —T-8.5:4

A Course in Miracles calls us to rise in love by dissolving the illusions that stand between us and the divine presence.

The Course doesn't advise us to go out and find someone to validate us. Or to keep fixing ourself until we become loveable. Or to identify the place on the planet where there is more love, and go there. The Course calls us to find love right where we stand, within us, just as we are. "Love remains the only present state, whose Source is here forever and forever." (W-293.1:2)

The healing journey does not require us to go anywhere. "You travel but in dreams, while safe at home." (T-13.VII.17:7) Healing is a movement of consciousness, elevating our vision to discover the well-being already bestowed. We can exchange belief in isolation for the recognition that we are always connected. Spirit is aware of any need, and will supply it.

My friend Audrey became quite ill, nearly immobilized. She prayed for a sign that God was with her. Then she took her dog to a dog park. There Audrey saw a tall, thin man wearing a white robe. He had long, flowing chestnut hair and a modest beard. He looked just like Jesus Christ. In that moment Audrey felt comforted, and the weight of her illness dropped away from her. "What do you think that experience was about?" she asked me.

"Jesus answered your prayer," I told her. "Perhaps, to give you solace, he manifested himself in a body. Or maybe he sent someone who looked just like him to remind you that he is with you. How it happened doesn't matter. The experience does."

If Jesus can show up in a dog park, he can find any of us wherever we are in the world. "When I said 'I am with you always,' I meant it literally. I am not absent to anyone in any situation." (T-7.III.1:7-8) While we may believe that love has forsaken us, the only real impossibility is that love is *not* where you stand.

The ecstatic Persian poets Rumi and Hafiz were drunk with divine love. They called God "the Beloved" and regarded their lives as a hide-and-seek game in which they had to pierce beyond the veils of earth to discover the Beloved. Our task—and reward—is the same. While we may seek a person to be our beloved, it is really our divine mate—our divine *Self*—that we seek. This is the mystical marriage that the sages speak of. John of the Cross advised, "Take God for your spouse and friend and walk with Him continually, and you will not sin and will learn to love, and the things you must do will work out prosperously for you."

Do you remember the first time you fell in love? What a marvelous experience! I met my first girlfriend just out of high school. I was so happy; my drab world was replaced with joy and heart. We spent the entire summer together, and the rest of the world disappeared. I wish I could bottle that experience and sip from it whenever I feel disconnected!

Then I went away to college, and we had a fight and broke up. The heady dream was over. The love was special love, not holy love. My life since that time has been a quest, with the help of *A Course in Miracles* and other penetrating teachings, to recapture that feeling without needing a person to incite it. Although that relationship did not last, the experience of love was real. "Only his love is real, and [God's Son] will be content

> The special love relationship is but a shabby substitute for what makes you whole in truth, not in illusion.
>
> —T-16.IV.8:4

only with his reality." (T-13.III.8:7) We all just want to be in love. How we get there makes all the difference in whether or not the experience will sustain.

While the world glorifies falling in love, our real adventure is to rise in love. Why would you want to descend when you can ascend? New age texts and teachers talk about "the ascension." The real ascension is not an event in time. It is attaining a state of mind. Rather than waiting for love to reveal itself at a future date, we are redirected to accept and celebrate the love already given. Jesus said, "Come, for all things are now ready" (Luke 14:17), including the love we have been seeking.

A fellow in one of my seminars asked, "How can I let in more love from my girlfriend?"

I told him, "You don't need to let more love in from your girlfriend. You need to let more love from within yourself out." We already own all the love we could ever want or need. We are like the musk deer, who searches the mountains and valleys for the source of an intoxicating aroma, only to discover that the scent is emanating from itself.

> If a mind perceives without love, it perceives an empty shell and is unaware of the spirit within.
>
> —T-I.IV.2:9

The search for love goes on until we are willing to find it. We must shift our identity from a spiritual seeker to a spiritual finder. "Every healer who searches fantasies for truth must be unhealed, because he does not know where to look for truth . . . " (T-9.V.2:3) The Course urges us to consider, "Do I want the problem or do I want the answer?" (T-11.VIII.4:6)

D.H. Lawrence masterfully expressed the same dynamic:

> Those that go searching for love
> only make manifest their own lovelessness,
> and the loveless never find love,
> only the loving find love,
> and they never have to seek for it.

When we go through a hard time, it may seem that love has deserted us. But it remains fully present; we are just not seeing it. As a young woman, Sandra went through a golden phase of life. "I fell in love, married, enjoyed a prosperous career, and felt totally alive," she told me. "Then, years later, things changed. I got divorced, my career fell apart, and I developed physical issues." Eventually Sandra met a wonderful fellow, started a new creative job, and she felt much better. "The golden time came around again," she explained.

Sandra thought for a moment and added, "Looking back now, I see that what I learned during my dark time matured me spiritually and prepared me for a new phase that went even deeper than my original golden time. So there was gold beneath the apparent emptiness."

At one time I was studying with two dynamic spiritual teachers who had joined forces. Then they had a falling out and parted ways. I felt disillusioned and confused. When I told a guru of my disappointment, he answered, "What kind of happiness was that? The two teachers were together, and you were happy. They parted, and you are unhappy. Why give the power of your happiness to any outer condition?"

Shakespeare put it inimitably:

> Love is not love which alters when it alteration finds,
> or bends with the remover to remove.
> O no, it is an ever-fixed mark that looks
> on tempests and is never shaken;
> it is the star to every wand'ring bark . . .

The ultimate awakening is to the love that we *are*. "The Kingdom of Heaven *is* you."(T-4.III.1:4) The reason it's so hard to find love in the outer world is that we are looking in the wrong place. You cannot travel to a kingdom you already carry within you. When Socrates implored us to "know thyself," he was not calling us to know our personality, body, or social media page. He was urging us to know ourselves as the embodiments of pure love.

The most fundamental love affair is with ourselves. External characters seem to show up, bring us love, and then depart. But they represent states of mind and heart we source from within. It is not narcissistic to fall (or rise) in love with yourself. Self-love is a prerequisite for loving others.

> Know yourself in the One Light where the miracle that is you is perfectly clear.
>
> —T-3. V.10:9

If God is love, and God is everywhere, then love must be everywhere. And if love is everywhere, it must be in you. You cannot be apart from what you are. Everything in nature finds ultimate fulfillment simply by being itself. In the world of illusion, people and events shift, making us believe we bob up and down with the winds and tides. But truth places us on solid ground, immovable by passing shadows. Forever we are held in the arms of love. There is really nowhere else to go.

> The still infinity of endless peace
> surrounds you gently in its soft embrace,
> so strong and quiet, tranquil in the might of its Creator,
> nothing can intrude upon the sacred Son of God within.
>
> –T-29.V.2:4

Miraculous Insights:

1. What do you think has to happen, or where do you think you need to go, to find happiness?
2. How might you find happiness right where you stand by changing your thoughts?
3. Have you ever had a prayer answered by someone showing up at the perfect time in the perfect way, and saying or doing something you needed to hear or see?
4. In what ways do you consider yourself a seeker?
5. How would you be thinking, feeling, and acting differently if you saw yourself as a finder?
6. How might the difficult or seemingly void times in your life have been an element of your highest good?
7. How would you be thinking, feeling, and acting differently if you knew you are loved just as you are, and you are on your perfect path?

Affirm:

Everything I need is given to me right where I stand.

I release my assumed identity as a seeker, and I claim my true identity as a finder.

Everything that happens to me is an element in the grand design of my highest good.

I am loved, supported, and healed here and now.

11

Don't Just Do Something—Stand There

Many of us are good at doing lots of things, but one thing we are not good at doing is nothing. Lots of people find stillness and silence terrifying, and flee from it. French mathematician and inventor Blaise Pascal said, "All human evil comes from a single cause, man's inability to sit still in a room."

My neighbor Roslyn could not be still for more than a few minutes. Her life was a constant stream of errands, shopping, and emergencies. I observed her car going in and out of her driveway many times a day. Then I got to know her. Roslyn was raised in a punitive religion, and she felt guilty about everything. If anything bad happened to anyone around her, she thought it was her fault. That helped me understand Roslyn's obsessive busyness—she was running from herself. She feared that if she sat and faced herself, she would find an ugly, evil person. Nothing could be farther from the truth. She was a kind, compassionate person—but her self-image was horrid. So she was always on the run.

A Course in Miracles graphically addresses this predicament: "Loudly the ego tells you not to look inward, for if you do your eyes will light on sin, and God will strike you blind.

This you believe, and so you do not look." (T-21.IV.2:3-4) Yet if we found the courage to face ourselves and pierce beyond the false veneer of evil, we would encounter a beautiful, holy, angelic being, with whom we would fall in love instantly and forever.

But most people do not afford themselves that space. Many avoid quiet like the plague. A sociological institute did a study of how long people can endure silence in a conversation before someone speaks to break the discomfort. That amount of time was three to four seconds. After that, the babble resumes.

I attended a church service at Princeton University where the spiritual master Sri Chinmoy was the guest speaker. At the appointed moment, the yogi stepped to the lectern, placed his hands together in *namaste* position, closed his eyes, and bowed his head. He retained that prayerful posture in silence for about twenty minutes. Then Sri Chinmoy opened his eyes, bowed, and stepped off the stage. That was one of the best sermons I have ever heard. The God of deep quietude delivered the message that morning.

Workbook lesson 106 asks us to pray, "Let me be still and listen to the truth." (W-106) We tend to assume that silence is empty, but it is extremely rich. Metaphysical teacher Joel Goldsmith wrote a book entitled, *The Thunder of Silence.* If you have ever truly dropped into silence, you know that it is extremely rich, a far more compelling statement than the empty static that often consumes our mind. Goldsmith urged his students, "Meditate until the meditation takes over." When I experience a deep meditation, I don't want to leave it. My sense of peace is so fulfilling that nothing I would get up for would be more rewarding. That is the power of deep stillness.

Silence paves the way for miracles. When I train holistic life coaches, I explain to them that silence and space are helpful elements of a coaching session. Usually after a long silent moment, the client will say something important. Quietude moves the client to reflect and ponder what would be the next meaningful thing to speak. I urge the coaches not to jump in to say something just because they feel pressured to keep the session moving along. Silence has motion in it. If you can relax while the wave goes out, the next wave will naturally come in.

> The miracle comes quietly into the mind that stops an instant and is still.
>
> —T-28.I.II:I

Silence also plays a major role in the cycles of our spiritual journey. All great masters retreat from activity and take refuge in stillness. Moses ascended to the summit of Mt. Sinai, where God dictated the Ten Commandments to him. While Mohammed meditated in Hira Cave, the Angel Gabriel gave him the Qur'an. Jesus sequestered himself in the desert for forty days, where he overcome three temptations hurled at him by the devil (aka ego). When each of these prophets emerged from their silent time, they delivered their world-changing teachings to humanity.

We enrich our lives and the lives of those we touch by following the example of those spiritual giants. In a world obsessed with busyness and often-distracting technology, we gain immense spiritual power when we step back, breathe deeply, and listen. Some organizations now offer "unplugged" retreats in which participants get away for a long weekend and renounce electronic communication. Could you go four days without your phone or computer? If not, your screen may be screening out peace. One of the "unplugged" programs touts the motto, "Disconnect to reconnect."

The slogan provides a potent summary of *A Course in Miracles'* call to quietude. When we disconnect from the world, we reconnect to Spirit. The Course tells us that either the body is real or Spirit is real, "For both you cannot have." (T-22.VI.1:2-3) You cannot simultaneously participate in noise and silence. There is a time for activity and a time for renewal. Self-nurturing is one of the most important contributions you can make to yourself, your loved ones, and the planet.

> Then wait a minute or so in silence, preferably with your eyes closed, and listen for His answer.
>
> —W-72.13:6

Silence is the womb through which guidance is birthed. If you have a decision to make, don't act hastily. In quiet, ask Holy Spirit what He would have you do. Acting from Spirit rather than ego will save you lots of time, trouble, and angst, and you will not have to go back and correct a faulty decision you made for the wrong reasons.

If you are seeking guidance, create a path for it to find its way to you. Imagine that the answers to all of your questions and problems are loaded onto an airplane about to land. You see the approaching craft, get excited, and dash onto the runway, waving your hands, yelling, "Here I am. Come on! Land already, would you?" Yet your scrambling about on the runway is precisely what is keeping the airplane from landing! If you would just step aside, take a seat, relax, and get quiet, you would clear the runway for the aircraft to deliver your gifts. "I will step back and let Him lead the way." (W-155)

Dropping into silence is especially effective when you have to make a decision as a couple or a group. Judy Skutch Whitson, who led the original publication of *A Course in Miracles*, tells that whenever the publishing team had a decision to make, everyone would get quiet and ask Holy Spirit for the answer. Invariable, Judy recounts, everyone came up with the same answer.

I once joined with ACIM teachers Michael and Maloah Stillwater to organize and present a retreat. Several months before the program, we reached the date when we had to pay the retreat center and guarantee a certain amount of attendees. But at that time we had just a few signups. If more people didn't register, we would sustain a huge loss. The three of us went round and round, discussing the pros and cons of taking the risk or withdrawing. Finally Maloah said, "Let's get quiet and ask for guidance." When we did, we all got the message to move ahead, and we paid the deposit. Soon afterward, lots of people signed up, and the retreat was filled.

Lesson 182 asks us to intend, "I will be still an instant and go home." (W-182) The introduction to the *Star Trek* television series declared, "Space: the final frontier." Yet outer space is not the final frontier. Inner space is. We can keep sending rockets, telescopes, probes, rovers, and people into outer space, but we will not find what we are looking for there. No matter how far we go, there will be a farther place. Only when we go in, will we find what we are looking for. Then we fulfill the Starship Enterprise's mission, "To boldly go where no man has gone before."

Diving into quietude is the most daring adventure, for it ". . . silences the thunder of the meaningless, and shows the way to peace to those who cannot see." (W-106.2:1) Stillness yields truth the intellect cannot embrace. It is said, "People invented words in order to lie." Where there are no words, there are no lies. Animals don't use words, and they never lie. Animals are completely authentic about who they are and what they want. People get muddled by words. To escape the tyranny of words, we must take refuge in the temple of silence.

What is the miracle that comes quietly to the still mind? The awareness that all is well; that you are whole; that God is present; and that you are enfolded in the arms of love. I know a spiritual teacher who asks his students to devote 30 minutes a day to meditation. He says, "That's 1/48 of your day. Isn't that a worthwhile investment to know God?" When you consider all the mindless activities that take up most of our waking hours, that's not a lot of time to neutralize insanity and replace it with the connection to Source that makes our lives worthwhile. Many people take great care and effort to make financial investments that yield a significant return. If we took the same diligence to invest our time wisely, we would be spiritual billionaires.

If you don't like formal meditation, engage in any activity that puts your mind into a receptive state. Walking in nature, painting, dancing, or playing music are valid spiritual practices. When your soul is at peace, you are meditating. Meditating changes the world far more powerfully than mechanical activity. Ernest Hemingway said, "Never mistake motion for action." Just because you are doing something doesn't mean you are getting anywhere. Immersing yourself in stillness leads to the most effective action. Action that proceeds from Source changes the world for the better. Action disconnected from Source perpetuates a frustrating world.

I saw a video of a group of people demonstrating against social injustice in an eastern European country. The protestors were simply standing quietly in the city square, eyes closed, absorbed in deep meditation and holding the intention for well-being and justice. Facing them stood a long line of policemen clad in riot gear. The policemen did not know what to do with the meditators. The police were armed for war. The protestors were armed for peace. It was obvious that the meditators were connected to a power far greater than the police. When I posted a clip of that scene on my Facebook page, it received more likes than any other post I have ever offered.

Moral of the story: Don't just do something. Stand there.

Miraculous Insights:

1. Can you sit quietly with yourself and enjoy your own company?
2. What fear keeps you from looking within?
3. What behaviors or habits do you use to distract yourself from being still?
4. How long can you endure silence in a conversation before you jump in to fill the space?
5. If you have a decision to make in a partnership or group, take time to get quiet together, go within, and ask for guidance. What guidance do you receive in common?
6. Would you be willing to commit to a regular meditation practice? If so, when would you meditate regularly, where, and how much time would you meditate?
7. If you don't enjoy or find success in formal meditation, what other activities do you engage in that yield you a sense of inner peace?

Affirm:

I regularly take time to be still,
go within, and connect with myself.

Spirit speaks to me clearly and
strongly in my quiet moments.

My meditation practice empowers
all of my activities and
my entire life.

12

Thank God My Neuroses are Irrelevant

When people ask me, "How has *A Course in Miracles* changed your life?" I sometimes feel embarrassed because, after 40 years of studying and teaching the Course, I have not fully mastered its lessons. Sometimes I feel like a beginner. I know a few ACIM teachers who claim that they no longer experience any fear or upset. Part of me envies them, another part wonders if they are telling the truth, and another part respects them for their attainment.

Yet behind ego's meanderings, I harbor an unspeakable appreciation for the gifts *A Course in Miracles* has brought to my life. How clearly I remember the night I opened my first copy and read the introduction. The words jumped out and electrified me like the Batman TV show exploded with a cartoon POW! when Batman punched a villain. As I stirred with the scintillating energy, a voice deep within me spoke: "This is real. This is important. Pay attention. Your soul is being called."

I have studied with many gifted teachers, healers, and channelers, and immersed myself in countless esoteric trainings. While all of these explorations have delivered rich blessings, scant few touch the overarching wisdom, depth, and unshakeable truth delivered through *A Course in Miracles*. I heard Judy Skutch Whitson say, "ACIM is a steep climb." It is like an express train that hurtles passengers to the ultimate destination without lots of local stops. When I co-presented a workshop with Neale Donald Walsch, author of the beloved *Conversations with God* series, a participant asked him, "Will you help me manifest a car?" Neale answered, "This isn't that kind of workshop."

Neither is ACIM that kind of workshop. There are two kinds of workshops: those that help you get stuff, and those that help you get peace. ACIM is door number two. It is not concerned with stuff. It is concerned with healing, specifically the healing of the mind. It is a steep climb because it makes no compromises and calls students to bypass goals that will fade and leave us wanting. It is unbending in its integrity and commitment to a full homecoming. If you would still like to take the local train, you can. But the journey will take longer and you will experience more ups, downs, and suffering. There is a far quicker and easier path to healing. "The miracle substitutes for learning that might have taken thousands of years" (T-1.II.6:7).

Just out of college I moved into a conservative neighborhood with four roommates. Our next door neighbor, Mrs. Ryan, was not exactly pleased as punch to have five young partiers next door. She found all kinds of things to complain about, we resisted, and our relationship grew quite strained.

Then one evening I attended a seminar in which the instructor asked the audience to call to mind someone we weren't getting along with. No problem—Mrs. Ryan's face came to me in a flash. "Now take a few moments to drop into your heart and find a place inside you that appreciates that person," he suggested. That was harder. But I did it. For the first time, I was able to feel a sense of acceptance and even *agape* for my neighbor. That sure felt better than being upset with her.

The next day while I was working in my garden, Mrs. Ryan approached the fence. "What's she going to complain about now?" I wondered. Instead, she said, "I know I haven't been the best neighbor. I'd like to start over and be friends with you guys." I almost dropped my tomatoes! Extending the olive branch was totally out of character with the Mrs. Ryan I knew. The interaction was nothing less than a miracle. Our relationship went on to be very harmonious.

I consider this event a scientific demonstration that when mind changes, so does the outer world. Nothing in our relationship changed except that for a few moments I found a place in my heart for her. But that was enough. "Your part is only to offer Him a little willingness to let Him remove all fear and hatred, and to be forgiven." (T-18.V.2:5)

A Course in Miracles has yielded me immense comfort of soul. When I read the Text, I feel that Jesus is holding me in his arms and assuring me, "Don't worry, everything will be alright." Studying the Text seems enigmatic because the language is uber-esoteric and appeals to the intellect. Yet I have often read passages that my thinking mind did not understand at all, but I felt unspeakably peaceful after reading them. Jesus has imbued the lofty verbiage with a soothing spiritual balm. The Text keeps the mind occupied while Christ feeds our soul. Voltaire said, "The art of medicine consists of amusing the patient while nature cures the disease." So it is with the Text.

In a rare YouTube recording ("Dr. Helen Schucman Comments Pt. 1"), the ACIM scribe admitted (tongue in cheek) that the Course appealed to her because she is a "literary snob." She acknowledged that many other courses teach the same principles in a much simpler way. The Course speaks to people of intellectual orientation who would not likely be caught in a remote monastery sitting *zazen*. Course author Jesus compassionately tosses us a pithy bone to chew on while we subconsciously absorb salvation. Maybe that's part of the teaching: Healing is far more vibrational than intellectual.

ACIM has bestowed me with the gift of rapid release. In olden days I would spend hours, days, weeks, or in some cases years stewing over some grievance. Now when upsets arise, I find my way back to clarity far more quickly. "I could see peace instead of this" (W-34) has served as a blessed spiritual accelerator for me. It reminds me that upset is a choice, and I can choose otherwise if I wish.

I have also learned to take back my power from people and situations to which I used to attribute my happiness. This process highlights the Course's unusual meaning of forgiveness: nothing outside me can save me or hurt me.

> You who perceive yourself as weak and frail, with futile hopes and devastated dreams, born but to die, to weep and suffer pain, hear this: All power is given unto you in earth and Heaven. There is nothing that you cannot do.
>
> —W-191.9:1-2

As I observe insane political shenanigans, mass hysteria over diseases going around, and frightening doomsday prophecies, I escape the fray by realizing that none of these illusions have anything to do with reality, nor can they touch my inner peace. My relationship with God does not depend on politics, medicine, the economy, the number of my social media followers, my books' rankings on Amazon, or how many more Christmas lights my neighbors have strung up than I have. Truth is rock solid, unassailed by passing appearances.

The Course has also helped my relationship with my body. I am very keen as to when the body looms dominant, and I am more able to detach from its demands. One day I stepped into the shower and found that my partner had changed the shower head to one with a weaker stream. I began to feel irritated, feeling victim to her poor choice that adversely affected me. Then I recalled the Course's question, "What plans do you make that do not involve [the body's] comfort or protection or enjoyment in some way?" (T-18.VII.1:2) "Which is more important?" I considered. "My relationship with my beloved or the shower head?" I eventually forgot entirely about the shower head's water pressure, and I grew free of the pressure of my grievance.

> You can escape the body if you choose.
>
> —W-91.5:5

More and more, I recognize that Spirit is the only true source of my providence. I have found endless applications of Workbook Lesson 50, "I am sustained by the love of God." I have lifted up to the light all the sources I once believed sustained me: relationship partners, doctors, money, the government, vitamins, knowing the right people, and more.

"External source" is an oxymoron. While Spirit can work though external channels, these channels *deliver* our good rather than *create* it.

Spirit does not recognize any external forces. "Outside" is not in God's vocabulary. One mind does not include contradictory parts. There are not two forces. There is one power, the power of God. What people call evil or the devil is simply the singular power of God, misused. The belief in two powers is a denial of the one power. The Force is already with us. We just need to learn to use it in our favor.

I have often tended to be impatient. I don't like standing in lines or waiting for stuff. The Course has helped me live more in the moment and not relegate my good to some future time. I use "waiting time" to look for miracles. While standing in line at the bank, I strike up a conversation with the person in front of me; in a traffic jam I listen to an inspirational recording; while waiting for my partner to emerge from the supermarket I meditate or pray for the folks exiting the store. I am practicing knowing that something good is happening even while I am tempted to wait for something better to happen.

> Delay does not matter in eternity, but it is tragic in time . . . Your place is only in eternity, where God Himself placed you forever.
>
> —T-5.VI.I:3. . . I:7

Even while I have judged myself as a lagging student of *A Course in Miracles*, I am not alone. Tamara Morgan, daughter of Judy Skutch Whitson, told me that her mom once formed a regular Course study gathering called the "Slow Learners Group." I had to laugh, since I consider Judy one who has mastered ACIM as deftly as anyone who has ever studied it. So if you feel that you deserve an ACIM dunce cap, you are in good company.

At the same time, I have gained some solace that I might actually be tapped into ACIM's truth. The Course tells us that if you give something to someone, their receiving it proves that you had it to give. Since I receive many notes of thanks and miracle reports from readers of my book *A Course in Miracles Made Easy* and viewers of my YouTube series on ACIM (@AlanCohenAuthor), I consider that I must have some understanding of the Course. Even while I walk the path of a human apparently in a body, cloaked with an often-erring personality, my true self remains perfectly connected with the divine. I am not waiting until I attain full Buddhahood to let God be God in me. Ram Dass said, "Spiritual masters are just as neurotic as the rest of us. But to them, their neuroses are irrelevant."

Which brings me to my final celebration of how ACIM has blessed my life: I have compassion for my humanity. I don't fight or judge my foibles and errors like I once did. I can love myself even with my *shtick* and trust that my godliness is fully intact even when I am not aware of it. Ego cares about ego, while Spirit cares only about Spirit.

> Nothing can reach spirit from the ego, and nothing can reach the ego from spirit.
>
> —T-4.I.2:6-7

Looking back on my journey through the illusion of time and space, I hold a handful of gifts of God as supremely precious to help me escape from pain and keep my head on straight amidst an orgy of illusion. *A Course in Miracles*, yoga, my esteemed mentors, my dear partner, and my dogs top the list. Even while we wander in a weird dream, truth has penetrated fantasy to redeem us. Although we have turned away from love, it will never turn away from us. Christians often cite John 3:16, "For God so loved the world that He gave His only begotten son . . ." We might state with equal gratitude, "God's Son so loved the world that he gave it *A Course in Miracles*."

Miraculous Insights:

1. How has practicing *A Course in Miracles* helped your life?
2. If you are not *A Course in Miracles* student, what spiritual practice has helped your life, and how?
3. What miraculous events have occurred in your life after you changed your thoughts?
4. If you knew that there is nothing you cannot do, what would you do?
5. For what negative quirks, habits, or neuroses do you judge yourself?
6. What if these objects of your judgments were quite small and unimportant relative to your overall spiritual mission in your life?

Affirm:

My spiritual practice significantly elevates the quality of my life.

My miracle thoughts create miraculous results.

My self-judgments are meaningless in the face of my spiritual mission.

13

Why Givers Never Lose

Depression is a major issue for many people. In the United States, 43 million adults take prescription antidepressants; six million in the United Kingdom. Many others feel depressed but do not take prescription drugs. Most of us have felt at least a little depressed at one time or another, or anxious about our future and the future of the world.

Dr. Jerry Jampolsky, one of the first teachers who proliferated *A Course in Miracles*, found a cure for his own depressive episodes. "When I started to feel down, I would go out and help someone. I felt better immediately," Jerry reported. Helping and depression cannot coexist because the love you give goes through you to get to the other person, and in the process you are healed. This dynamic demonstrates ACIM's teaching that giving and receiving are the same; what you give, you receive the moment you give it.

> All that I give is given to myself.
>
> —W-126

The ego defines itself as empty and lacking, and is consistently making deals to get something from the outer world to fill in its bottomless void. By now you have begun to realize that this plan does not work. Because the ego's belief in lack is illusory, nothing it does to offset that lack will succeed. You cannot get a true result from a false premise. You cannot fill in something that is whole. The ego gives now to get later, and in the process misses the joy that genuine giving delivers at the moment of extension.

Years ago, I was sharing my finances with a partner who wanted to take an expensive healing training. The tuition was high, and she would have to travel extensively to participate in the classes. As I looked at the price tab, I balked, fearing that the cost would run down our assets. Upset ensued, and we argued.

That night I dreamt I was at a party serving spaghetti at a buffet. As the line of guests passed by and the spaghetti was getting down to the bottom of the pot, I feared that I would run out of pasta. But then I found that no matter how many people I served, when I dipped the ladle into the pot, there was enough to keep feeding people. Upon awakening, I realized that Spirit had given me this dream to offset my fear of lack of money. With newfound trust in infinite supply, I told my partner I would be happy to support her to take the training, and our relationship was restored to loving harmony.

The ego's gifts are material commodities, usually money and objects. There is a giver and a receiver; the giver loses and the receiver gains. Yet ACIM tells us that if anyone loses in a transaction, it is not a healthy one. ". . . If you choose to take a thing away from someone else, you will have nothing left. This is because, when you deny his right to everything, you have denied your own" (W-133:7:1-2) Right transactions lead to a win-win. The Holy Spirit's gifts are not material objects but energies, states of mind, and experience. When you give love, you don't have less love; you have more. When you forgive, you feel forgiven. Ideas do not diminish when you share them. They only expand, as the flame of a candle is not lessened when it lights another candle. There is only more light.

Real healing does not cost the healer. I saw a movie in which Jesus was depicted as returning to the world as a modern man, incognito. When he healed someone, he would wince and grab the side of his waist as if he had been stabbed. The movie's scriptwriter did not understand how healing works. In real life, Jesus did not incur pain by giving; his own wellness *increased*. Losing through healing is an old sacrifice-based paradigm that *A Course in Miracles* wants us to get over. Healing empowers the healer as much as the recipient. If you feel depleted after you help or heal someone, there is an error in your mental formula. Either you believe that you are the healer rather than the Holy Spirit working through you, or you believe that you have to lose for someone else to gain. But you do not need to die for someone else to live. Life cannot come from death. Life comes only from life.

This dynamic is as real and alive today for us as it was for Jesus. Giving a gift of God energizes everyone involved. When I write a book, teach a class, or coach a client, I am never tired afterward. I have more energy than when I began. If you feel depleted when helping someone, you may be holding some subconscious belief in decrease as a path to increase. Raise that belief up to the light, and you will realize that no one loses through giving.

The famous Prayer of St. Francis asks us to remember, "It is in giving that we receive; it is in pardoning that we are pardoned." Eight hundred years ago, the gentle mystic tapped into the very principle that Jesus illuminates in *A Course in Miracles*. There is no time delay between giving and receiving. You receive at the moment you give.

Being a good receiver is as important as being a good giver. Many people on the spiritual path are generous with others, but resist receiving. Their equation is out of balance. When you accept a material or spiritual gift from someone, you are helping them receive the reward they reap through giving. If you resist their gift, you deprive them of the joy of giving. In receiving, you are giving.

My mentor Hilda made sophisticated use of this principle. When someone complimented her, for example, "That was a great lecture, Hilda," she would not simply say, "Thank you." She would respond, "Did you really like it?" Then the speaker would go on about the benefits she had received from the lecture.

Hilda was not insecure, and she was not fishing for compliments; she was one of the most egoless people I have ever met. In asking the speaker, "Did you really like it?" she was giving the speaker the opportunity to express more about what she had received, lifting and empowering her as she gave more appreciation.

Hilda would occasionally lead a meditation on the theme of gratitude. She asked us to think of all the people in our life that we appreciate. Then she added, "Include me in your gratitude list. I don't need your thanks, but you need to give it." She was teaching that giving gratitude is more important than receiving it.

There is a simple way to differentiate between the gifts of the ego and the gifts of God: If you have less after giving, your gift was ego-driven. If you have more after giving, the gift was spirit-driven. The ego and the Holy Spirit agree that they want us to accumulate treasures. But they do not agree on the kind of treasures they want us to accumulate. The ego wants us to amass entities like physical possessions and worldly accolades. The Holy Spirit wants us to accumulate inner peace and well-being.

> My treasure house is full, and angels watch its open doors that not one gift is lost, and only more are added.
>
> —W-316:4

Jesus taught, "Judge not, so you are not judged." Most people interpret this teaching as, "If you judge now, God will judge you later." The dynamic is much simpler. When you judge a person or event, you drop into the consciousness of judgment, a state of mind in which everything is condemnable—including yourself. We reap the results of the kind of vision we use to see the world, for better or worse. Love sees beauty and worth everywhere, and fear sees ugliness and error everywhere. We might paraphrase Jesus's teaching, "When you hold grievances against the world, you will automatically hold grievances against yourself." The ego attempts to exclude you from grievances by projecting them outward, but guilt will still hold its grip on you. The only way to escape judgment is to release the world. "Only my condemnation injures me. Only my own forgiveness sets me free." (W-198.9:3-4)

The Course offers a striking metaphor: When you keep someone in the prison of your judgments, you have to sit at the door of their cell to make sure they do not escape.

> A jailer is not free, for he is bound together with his prisoner. He must be sure that he does not escape, and so he spends his time in keeping watch on him. The bars that limit him become the world in which his jailer lives, along with him. And it is on his freedom that the way to liberty depends for both of them.
>
> —W-198:3-6

Your gifts to the world are your gifts to yourself. "To have, give all to all." (T-6.V.A.) You cannot outgive God. For as much as you give, there is more in store for you to give to others and receive for yourself. The more you focus on an idea, the larger it grows. When you recognize the blessings you already own, they expand.

God does not want anyone to be depressed, guilty, or fearful. Those are all attributes of the world the ego has manufactured. While many people are helped by prescription antidepressants, the most powerful antidepressant is love. One of my coaching clients reported that she daily visited her father in the hospital. She had brought him an aromatherapy unit to diffuse healing scents in the room. "Is there anything else I could do for him?" she asked me.

I told her, "*You* are the master diffuser. When you enter his presence with joy and genuine love in your heart, you are diffusing high vibrations that go far beyond what the mechanic diffuser is radiating."

Giving and receiving love are the same. You cannot give love without receiving it, and you cannot receive love without giving it. Jesus did not wince when he gave love, and neither do we need to. The entire Course in Miracles is a gift of love, and the more we practice it, the more love there is in the world for all of us.

Miraculous Insights:

1. Have you ever felt depressed? If so, what helped free you?
2. Do you ever argue with your spouse or someone else about money?
3. If so, what lack thoughts are fueling your argument?
4. What thoughts of abundance would release your fear of lack, and end your argument?
5. What is the difference between the gifts of the ego and the gifts of the spirit?
6. If you are a teacher or healer, do you ever feel depleted or drained after teaching or healing?
7. What belief do you hold that implies you must lose for someone else to gain?
8. Would you be willing to question or challenge your belief in sacrifice, and replace it with a win-win model?
9. How do your judgments keep you in prison?
10. How does your forgiveness free you?

Affirm:

I elevate myself by choosing thoughts of abundance and generosity.

My teaching and healing empowers me along with my students and clients.

Releasing others is my gift to myself as well as them.

14

How Long Would You Like to Be Happy For?

If you want to be happy for an hour—take a nap.
If you want to be happy for a day—go fishing.
If you want to be happy for a month—get married.
If you want to be happy for a year—inherit a fortune.
If you want to be happy for a lifetime—help someone.

This ancient Chinese proverb captures the heart of *A Course in Miracles*. The happiness the world provides is fleeting. Peace that depends on outer events goes as quickly as it came. Yet there is another kind of peace that lasts forever. Jesus said, "My peace I give unto you, not as the world gives, give I unto you." (John 14:27) What the world gives, goes away. What God gives, lives for eternity.

> And truth stands radiant,
> apart from conflict,
> untouched and quiet
> in the peace of God.
>
> —T-23.I.7:10

If we want the peace of God, we have to focus exclusively on it. Divided attention undermines reaching the goal.

You can't immerse yourself in war, horror, or crime movies, or the news (the same thing) and retain the peace of God. "Peace is impossible to those who look on war." (M-11.4:1) I know people who sat and watched the news constantly during the Covid pandemic. They became nervous wrecks. I also know people who meditated constantly during the pandemic. They became a force for healing.

There is an even more subtle teaching here. It is not movies, or the news, or annoying people that remove our peace. The real culprits are the judgments we hold when we look upon them, and the fears we indulge. It is possible to look upon anything the world shows us, no matter how dark or grisly, and maintain our peace if we are committed to it. Conflict in the world is a projection of the conflict we perceive within ourselves. If we wish to stop wars on Earth, we must first stop the wars in our mind.

An advanced soul could stand in the midst of a battleground and remain at peace. During a war in Lebanon, Mother Teresa learned of a children's hospital in Beirut that was threatened by gunfire and bombs. This saintly soul announced that she and a group of her nuns would drive into that city to rescue the children and transport them to a safe location. When the warring factions learned of her mission, they declared a cease-fire. I was amazed as I watched a video of Mother Teresa leading a caravan of Red Cross trucks through the streets of the city. Soldiers from the opposing armies stood silently, guns down. When the nuns had accomplished their task, they drove out of the city, and the armies went back to fighting.

Mother Teresa's consciousness was so established in well-being, compassion, and trust that she created a psychic

> Peace is inevitable to those who offer peace.
>
> —M-11.4:2

sphere of safety around her staff and the children. She literally stopped a war. "What else but a Thought of God turns hell to Heaven merely by being what it is? The earth bows down before its gracious Presence, and it leans down in answer, to raise it up again." (M-11.4:9-10)

When you are founded in peace, not only do you not see war, but you are invisible to those who choose war. My friend Keith was sitting in a fast-food restaurant with his friend, talking about consciousness and experience. "If we were firmly established in a peaceful state of mind, that building right next to us could blow up and we would not even notice it," Keith said to his buddy.

Minutes later, the two men were interrupted by policemen storming their table and ordering them to stand and be frisked. While the two had been immersed in their spiritual conversation, two crooks had robbed the restaurant at gunpoint. All the other customers ran out. But Keith and his friend were so engaged in their higher consciousness discussion that they were not even aware of the robbery, and the thieves did not see them. They were absorbed in a reality quite discontinuous with the one in which there was a robbery and potential violence or danger.

Peace does not fight war. It simply remains itself, and in so doing, undoes war. "So does [the ego] do constant battle with the Holy Spirit about what your happiness is. It is not a two-way battle. The ego attacks and the Holy Spirit does not respond." (W-66.2:2-4) The ego's thoughts are based on attack, whether we see ourselves as attacked or attacking, and the Holy Spirit's thoughts are founded in forgiveness and

> I can escape from the world I see by giving up attack thoughts.
>
> —W-23

release. We win the battles of life not by getting rid of our opponents, but by walking off the battlefield. When Mother Teresa was invited to speak at an anti-war rally, she declined. "Fighting war is just another form of war," she explained. "If this were a pro-peace rally, I would gladly participate."

A part of us remains at peace even while the ego goes through its crazy shenanigans. Our true self is unmoved regardless of changes at the surface level of our experience. That self is awake even while the ego is bogged in a stupor. We will not find healing by rearranging the characters and props in a dream of conflict. We will find healing only by waking from the dream.

> Now we see that darkness is our own imagining, and light is there for us to look upon. Christ's vision changes darkness into light, for fear must disappear when love has come. Let me forgive Your holy world today, that I may look upon its holiness and understand it but reflects my own.
>
> —W-302.1:5-7

A student new to ACIM asked me how to respond to her friends who criticize her for not watching the news anymore, and refusing to engage in gossip or political arguments. They told her, "You are living in a dream world."

I explained to her that *everyone* is living in the dream world of their choice, including her friends. Each of us believes that our dream is real and everyone else's dream is fake. Insecure people deny the dreams of others in order to bolster their own. During the Covid pandemic, I saw a magazine cover showing a person with his head in the sand, suggesting that people who were not worried about Covid were in denial. Yet people who were worried about Covid were also in denial. Any form of worry is a denial of peace. Bill Watterson's Calvin of *Calvin and Hobbes* declared, "It's not denial. I'm just selective about the reality I accept."

Metaphysical teachers often talk about the importance of affirmations, while the more advanced teachers underscore the power of denials. To gain the reality of wholeness, we must deny the *apparent* reality of fragmentation. *A Course in Miracles* includes lots of denials. "I am not a body. I am free." (W-199) "There is no death. The son of God is free." (W-163) "True denial is a powerful protective device. You can and should deny any belief that error can hurt you. This kind of denial is not a concealment but a correction. Your right mind depends on it." (T-2.II.2:1-4)

Advocates of war say that if we avoid conflict we are running away from reality. But if we avoid peace we are running away from reality. Ram Dass used to say that if you are angry or upset in your attempts to bring peace to the world, you are sending out waves of vibrations that cause war. Abraham-Hicks teaches that people who form organizations to fight something usually end up fighting amongst themselves. People who come together to extend peace end up being more peaceful.

Because the world of ego is built on conflict, it is disarmed when it encounters peace. Healing does not call us to fight the ego, but to choose peace instead. ". . .You cannot escape from the ego by humbling it or controlling it or punishing it." (T-4.VI.3:8) If you fight the ego, the ego has won because fighting feeds it. We get rid of ego not by battling it, but by refusing to indulge it.

A Native American tribesman told his medicine man, "There are two wolves fighting in my head. One is dark and aggressive, and the other is light and peaceful. Which one will win?"

"The light one will win," the medicine man replied.

"Why is that?" the young man asked.

"That is the one you will feed."

Peace is the great need of the world because peace is the great need of our mind. The first step to a world at peace is a mind at peace. It's impossible to see a peaceful world through a troubled mind. ACIM continually advises us to withdraw our efforts to change conditions around us, and instead to upgrade the vision we are using.

> And can the world be saved if you are not?
> —W-20.3:5

In some of my seminars I give participants a small mirror and instruct each of them to mess up their hair. Then I ask them to touch the mirror and try to fix their hair. They cannot do it, and they laugh. The mirror simply reflects the hair; it does not cause it. If you want to fix your hair, you need to manipulate your hair, not its reflection. All outer change begins with a change of mind.

A nap, fishing, marriage, or inheritance yields momentary respite from the pain that living in illusion engenders. *A Course in Miracles* would have us escape from pain not by substituting one illusion for another, but by substituting reality for illusion. The only real escape is into truth. The Course tells us, "All real pleasure comes from doing

God's Will." (T-1.VII.1:4) God's will is for us to be happy—not by importing experiences, but by realizing that happiness is seeded deep within us. In the world, peace seems abnormal and unnatural. But the world is inside out and upside down. The Peace of God is the most natural experience to a divine being, and it lasts forever.

> Yet you can ask as easily for love, for happiness,
> and for eternal life in peace that has no ending.
> Ask for this, and you can only win.
>
> –W-200.3:1-2

Miraculous Insights:

1. What things do you want that are temporary and will fade with time?
2. What do you want that is eternal and will not fade with time?
3. What problems, diseases, conflicts, or wars do you give your attention to, and how does that make you feel?
4. What beauty, love, abundance, health, and peace do you give your attention to, and how does that make you feel?
5. When you try to change other people or the world, how does that leave you feeling frustrated?
6. When you change your mind about other people or the world, how does that bring you peace?

Affirm:

I find inner peace by
valuing what is eternal.

I give my full attention to
the blessings in my life.

I do not need to manipulate
to become peaceful.

I gain the deepest well-being
by changing my mind.

15

Clouds Cannot Stop You

When Christopher Columbus's three ships approached the island of Guanahani in the Caribbean, the natives standing on the beach didn't see the ships. They had never seen clipper ships before. The idea of such a vessel did not live in their mind or their reality, so those forms were invisible to the natives. We see only what we believe in. It's possible to miss something right in front of you because you don't believe it's there—or your attention is elsewhere.

In my seminars I show a video of two small teams of college students, one wearing white T-shirts, the other, black T-shirts. Both teams are standing in a circle, passing a basketball to members of their own team. I ask the viewers to count the number of passes the white team makes during a 30-second period. I even offer them a prize if they state the correct number. Afterward I ask the audience if they have any comments on the video.

One or two viewers ask, "What's up with that gorilla that walked through the group?"

"What gorilla?" I playfully reply.

"Someone in a gorilla costume walked into the midst of the basketball players, faced the camera, pounded its chest, and walked out of the room."

"That's really weird," I say. "Let's have another look at the video." I replay the video, and, sure enough, a person in a gorilla suit made a bold appearance.

The viewers who did not see the gorilla—about two-thirds of the audience—are astonished. They ask, "Is that the same video you showed us the first time?"

It certainly is. This psychology experiment illustrates a principle called "inattentional blindness." Because the viewers were so focused on counting basketball passes, they did not see the gorilla. They were very aware of what they were paying attention to, and unaware of what they were not paying attention to. This is clear demonstration of the Law of Perception. (YouTube: "Selective Attention Test from Simon and Chabris 1999")

You may experience the same phenomenon at home in the form of "fridge blindness." You open the door of the refrigerator, looking for a jar of mayonnaise, and you don't find any. "Did we finish the mayo, hon?" you call out in frustration. Your spouse walks to the refrigerator, reaches to the jar of mayonnaise right in front of you, and hands it to you. You stand there, embarrassed. Maybe you thought the mayo was not there. Or you were looking elsewhere. Or your mind was on another subject. But it was right in front of you the whole time.

A Course in Miracles guides us to redirect our attention from grievances to gratitude. Like the clipper ships, gorilla, and mayonnaise, it's possible to miss love because you are looking elsewhere. That tragic misperception is not just common—it's the human condition. It is said, "Many people are good at counting the cost, but few are good at counting the benefits."

Lots of people complain about struggling with writer's block or a similar artistic impediment. I prefer to substitute the word "distraction" for "block." A "block" sounds solid and impenetrable, like the imposing monolith the prehistoric apes encountered in the movie, *2001: A Space Odyssey*. Such massive forms are dense and formidable. Are our life lessons really that thick? Is the reality built on faulty perception made of cement? Do we need a jackhammer to demolish those obstructions? Or might we move past perceived challenges quickly, gracefully, and easily, by shifting to a higher vision rather than remaining fixated on the problem?

We do not need to sweat to hack away at illusions. We are stronger than they are. Workbook Lesson 69 gives us soothing imagery to help us transcend apparent obstacles. Jesus asks us to imagine rising through clouds that obscure our view of the sun. "Determine to go past the clouds," he suggests. "Brush them aside with your hand; feel them resting on your cheeks and forehead and eyelids as you go through them. Go on; clouds cannot stop you." (W-69.6:4-5) Rising through the mist of unsubstantial clouds is a lot easier than trying to demolish massive blocks.

Love is always present, but we are not. Energy flows where attention goes. When we give our attention to illusions, we miss the truth. We dwell in the realm equivalent to our consciousness. Jesus explained this dynamic in the language of his time: "In my Father's mansion there are many rooms." (John 14:2) There are an infinite number of chambers of consciousness in this sprawling universe. Every thought we think is a key that opens the door to a unique room. When we become fearful, we enter the room that contains all things fearful. When we focus on love, we gain access to all that is loving. Awakening is a lot simpler than we've been told. We just need to keep our attention on what our spirit values, not the ego's bogus prizes.

The world of fear is unsubstantial and requires no resistance. We do not need to spend time and energy fighting sin. What we fight, we magnify in our experience. If we try to crash through our perceived blocks, we will get banged and bruised. The way to defeat the physical world is to rise above it. Jesus said, "In the world you shall have tribulation. But take heart, for I have overcome the world." (John 16:33) In ACIM he reiterates that when we finally win the battle against sin, we will realize that battle was never required; we could have simply said, "I have no use for this." (M-5.II.2:12) Then behaviors that we deem sinful would just fall away due to our lack of interest.

Every year I host a Hawaii retreat for Japanese participants. The Japanese are very obedient people, trained to follow the rules their culture has set for them. A lot of my work with them is to help them trust themselves and their inner guidance. During one retreat a young woman told me, "I just got divorced, and I am ready to start dating again. I would like to have three boyfriends, but I feel guilty."

"You are allowed to have as many boyfriends as you like," I told her. "There is no rule about how many boyfriends you can have." She was thrilled to hear this, and thanked me profusely.

Another fellow told me, "I had an argument with my father, and I don't want to speak to him."

I told him, "That's fine. Maybe it would serve you not to speak with him for a while." He liked that idea, and also thanked me profusely.

When I next visited Japan, I saw both of these students. The woman told me, "I decided all I really want is one boyfriend. So that's what I have, and I am happy with him." The fellow told me, "After a while I missed speaking to my dad, and we made amends. Our relationship is really good now."

In both of these cases, the clients were simply looking for permission to do what they wanted to do. It was not my permission they needed, but their own. When they flowed with their intentions, life found a way to balance them out. I knew that the woman would not do well with several boyfriends, and the fellow would eventually reconcile with his dad. But they each needed to make their own decision and learn from its results.

The ancient Chinese art of *Wu Wei* teaches the value of "effortless action." When we do not fight ourselves, other people, or the universe, we arrive at the highest result. Flowing with your inner guidance rather than bucking through obstacles yields success and inner peace. In the ACIM passage, Jesus is not calling us to buck through the clouds, but instead to gently rise above them. If you are trying to break a bad habit, self-judgment and resistance keep it in force. Guilt compels you to continue to do what you feel guilty about. "What you resist, expands and persists." *A Course in Miracles* tells us that guilt is never an appropriate view of anyone's behavior, including your own. Forgiveness will progress you far more efficiently than guilt. Instead of fighting your bad habits, focus on other activities that elevate you to a higher vibration. Then the bad habit will fall away and you will graduate from it. Twelve-step programs are effective because members take hold of a Higher Power, which lifts them beyond their addiction. The idea of being a "spiritual warrior" is an oxymoron. Only the ego is at war. Meanwhile Spirit looks on lovingly, patiently waiting for the warrior to drop his weaponry so he can ascend beyond the misty veils of the appearance of separation.

The Holy Spirit and the ego are like radio stations, each broadcasting at a unique frequency. If you are listening to a radio playing loud annoying music or constantly blaring bad news, you don't need to argue with the radio, smash it with a hammer, or form a support group for people who have been victimized by the negative vibes. You simply need to switch the channel so you attune to a more desirable station with soothing music and uplifting words. Station KGOD is broadcasting 24/7. We just need to set our dial so we can receive it.

Even the idea of "breakthrough" implies there is an obstacle formidable enough to break through. Breaking anything is a form of violence. The Manual for Teachers tells us that one of the attributes of a Teacher of God is gentleness. Gentleness does not wrestle. It transcends. If you find yourself wrestling with anyone or anything, stop, step back, breathe, and ask, "What would gentleness do here?" You don't have to kill your ego. To kill anything is an act of violence. Only ego tries to kill ego. Spirit simply sees through the ego into the reality of love.

If you are preoccupied trying to get rid of your demons, you will only find more demons to vanquish. Living in a demon-filled world is the result of immersing yourself in demon consciousness. What you fight, you feed. Quit trying to fix your faults or fill in your emptiness. Jesus said, "Be perfect even as your Father in heaven is perfect." (Matthew 5:48) He didn't say, "Become perfect." You can't become perfect because God has already created you perfect. After you have exhausted all efforts to fix yourself, you will realize that the real you never needed fixing.

The idea of self-improvement is also an oxymoron. Your true Self cannot be improved on. You cannot get to wholeness by focusing on brokenness. You cannot get to truth by way of illusion. The one doing the fixing is the same one that needs to be fixed. The fox is in charge of the henhouse. Quit identifying yourself as fault-ridden, and identify instead as a being of light. *Disown dysfunction*. Quirks may leave or they may stay. In either case, they will not matter because you are established in your higher nature.

> You cannot be your guide to miracles for it is you who made them necessary.
>
> –T-14.XI.7:1

A Course in Miracles helps us dissolve apparent obstacles by first showing us that they are unsubstantial, and then by making love so attractive that we would rather pay attention to it instead of fear. Fear ultimately fails because it is not of God, and therefore not formidable. Only love is real. All else is just a weird dream from which love helps us awaken.

Miraculous Insights:

1. What evil or negativity are you battling in yourself, others, or the world?
2. Can you see how fighting anything reinforces what you are fighting?
3. How might you come to genuine peace by releasing your resistance and gently rising above it?
4. What permission are you seeking from the outer world to do something you would like to do?
5. Who do you think you need permission from?
6. Can you give yourself the permission you were seeking from others?
7. How would you be living your life differently if you gave up any sense of struggle and allowed your actions to flow from ease and joy?

Affirm:

I release any need to
fight for my good.

A benevolent universe
generously provides all I need.

I give myself permission to have and
do the things that bring me true joy.

I can flow with life because
I am blessed as a child of God.

16

Closer to Morning than You Know

While I was in college, my girlfriend and I flew to Puerto Rico to attend a rock festival. We camped on the beach with thousands of stoned partiers, and cavorted naked under the full moon. We were under no laws but God's long before *A Course in Miracles* told us so.

One night after my girlfriend fell asleep in our tent, I did something incredibly stupid. I walked along the beach, held out my hand, and accepted all kinds of drugs and liquor from people I didn't know. Then I downed it all. It was not long before I tailspinned into a paranoid hallucination. I believed that some local guys who had been hanging around the festival had raped and killed my girlfriend, and they were on their way to kill me. This bad trip sucked me into a night of the deepest and darkest hell; I was sure I would never see the light of day again.

You can imagine my relief when hours later I found myself sitting on a rock watching the sun rising over the ocean. The effects of the drugs had worn off; none of what I feared had happened, and I reclaimed my sanity. I will never forget watching the first rays of light touching the sky, and realizing, "That was all just a very bad dream."

> You do not walk alone. God's angels hover near and all about. His Love surrounds you, and of this be sure; that I will never leave you comfortless.
>
> —W-ep.6:6-8

Years later I opened *A Course in Miracles* to Lesson 169 and read, "By grace I live. By grace I am released." Then I realized that my angels were on the job that night. Jesus assures us that we will wake up from the nightmares that have ravaged our lives, and emerge unscathed. "The end of dreams is promised me, because God's Son is not abandoned by His Love." (W-279.1:1)

Sometimes we have to go through a dark night of the soul to get to the light. The deeper the darkness, the brighter the light it reveals. The greater the contraction, the more the subsequent expansion. If you toss a rubber ball against the floor gently, it will bounce a little. If you throw it hard, the greater force at the point of impact will send the ball to a loftier height. Likewise, our most difficult hardships can lead to the greatest transformations. We might curse hard times as we move through them, but when we later look back on them and realize how they helped us grow, we thank them. Every miracle begins with a problem and ends with a blessing.

By the time Starr Daily was nineteen years old, he had committed so many bank robberies that he was sentenced to many years of imprisonment. In jail, he was a constant troublemaker, defying the guards and inciting riots. Before long he was locked in solitary confinement, hanging from his wrists all day long, and sleeping on a cement floor at night. When the guards came to deliver his meals, he spat in their faces. The depth to which this soul had sunk was unspeakable.

Then an extraordinary event occurred. As Daily was near death due to his horrendous conditions and malnourishment, Jesus Christ appeared to him and permeated him with unconditional love. "I could feel evil draining out of my body," Daily recounted. After that experience he was a changed man. He became a model prisoner, studied and taught the Bible, and wrote two inspiring books, *Release* and *Love Can Open Prison Doors*.

> Darkness and turmoil and death have disappeared. The light has come.
>
> —W-75.I.6-7

While light often follows darkness, light already exists behind the curtain of evil. When American troops liberated a Nazi concentration camp at the end of World War II, they found most prisoners emaciated, sick, and near death. Yet amidst this demoralized group they encountered one man who looked robust, healthy, and happy. "Are you a recent arrival here?" the liberators asked him. "No, I have been here the whole time," he answered. Even in the midst of horrific conditions, this man found a way to retain his well-being. I find this a striking inspiration that we, whose daily challenges are far lighter, can rise above the fray and choose well-being. "Let our gratitude unto our Teacher fill our hearts, as we are free to choose our joy instead of pain, our holiness in place of sin, the peace of God instead of conflict, and the light of Heaven for the darkness of the world." (W-190.11:2)

We can reframe dense darkness as a sign that we are getting close to the light. There is a fascinating psychobiological phenomenon called the *extinction burst*. If you give a dog a treat every time it whines, when you withhold the treat, the dog's whining will intensify. This moment is a crucial one for the dog's trainer. If you give in to the bad behavior, it will continue. But if you can resist the temptation to give in, eventually the dog will realize that the old behavior will not obtain its reward, and it will give up. (Often the dog's person needs to be trained more than the dog!)

The ego is the old whining behavior that at one time received payoffs for upset, complaining, and warfare. Enter *A Course in Miracles*, which encourages us to reach for a higher reward. At this point, the old ego behaviors or habits rear up and make a huge stink. If we give in, the ego wins and the pattern goes on. If we refuse to give in, the ego will subside and we will rise to higher ground.

> Forget not now the misery you really found, and do not breathe life into your failing ego.
>
> —T-17.V.8:4-5

Regarding ego flareups as extinction bursts gives us leverage to move past them. Psychic tantrums are a sign that you are making progress. If you were still trapped in the ego's world of false limits, "the lion sleeps tonight." But when the ego perceives its fear-based domain is being threatened, the lion awakens and roars. Fundamentalists say, "the more precious you are to God, the more precious you are to the devil." The closer you come to the light, the more vehemently the darkness attempts to engulf you. In truth, the darkness has no volition, power, or reality. But the part of our mind that finds value in darkness can make darkness seem formidable.

While darkness may signal the coming of the light, we may be tempted to believe that suffering is a ticket to heaven. "No pain, no gain" is a popular maxim cited by religious teachers and athletic coaches. Yet *A Course in Miracles* might substitute, "No pain, no pain." The Course does not want us to glorify pain, but rather to withdraw our value in it. "Learning through rewards is more effective than learning through pain, because pain is an ego illusion, and can never induce more than a temporary effect. The rewards of God, however, are immediately recognized as eternal." (T-4.VI.3:4-5)

In the Text section "The Message of the Crucifixion," Jesus asks us to drop the old rugged cross and not repeat the trials he endured. He explains that his experience on the cross was an extreme teaching in forgiveness. If he could forgive the brutal treatment he received, we can certainly forgive in far less trying circumstances. Over and over and over again, Jesus calls us to withdraw our consciousness from the world of sorrow, and establish our mind in peace. Self-mutilation and glorifying suffering do not befit our identity as divine beings.

God's will for me is perfect happiness.

—W-101

We may also be prone to believe that the longer we suffer, the greater the reward when we find the light, so we unnecessarily prolong suffering. *"This need not be."* (T-4.IV) Imagine two rooms: One has been dark for ten years, and the other has been dark for ten minutes. When you switch on the light in both rooms, which room is illuminated faster? Both rooms become lighted immediately. It does not matter how long or how deep the room has been immersed in darkness.

The moment the light comes, both rooms are equally filled with light. "Love waits on welcome, not on time, and the real world is but your welcome of what always was." (T-13.VII.9:7)

Neither does it matter how long you have been sick, broke, depressed, or in a dysfunctional relationship. Being ill for ten years does not mean you require ten years to heal. You can heal in a moment. The Apostle Paul said, "In a moment, in the twinkling of an eye . . . we shall be changed." (1 Corinthians 15:52) Many people have instantaneous spontaneous remissions. Supposedly at death's door, they have a shift in consciousness that restores them to full health. Doctors may cite prognoses of a long recovery period, or none at all. But "I am under no laws but God's." (W-76) Doctors make predictions on the basis of their personal experiences and statistics. Yet personal experiences are based on personal belief systems, which a Son of God is not required to share. Statistics apply to masses of people, not individuals. If you participate in the consciousness of the masses, you will have the same experience. The Son of God is not subject to mass beliefs. You are subject only to the Grace of God, which is freely and eternally given.

The journey from darkness to light is not one of time, distance, or action. It is a shift in perception. Waiting is a state of mind that generates more waiting. Finding generates more finding. "Time is the great illusion [heaven] is past or in the future. Yet this cannot be, if it is where God wills His Son to be. How could the Will of God be in the past, or yet to happen? What He wills is now . . ." (W-131.6:1-6)

Winston Churchill said, "When walking through hell, keep going." That great statesman nobly guided the United Kingdom through the horrors of World War II. Tragic as that epoch was, the country and the world emerged once again into light. Emergence in time is one thing; emergence in consciousness is another. *A Course in Miracles* wants us to lift our vision above darkness and war entirely. If we can keep our eyes on inner light in the face of outer darkness, we are true Teachers of God. We are closer to morning than we know.

Miraculous Insights:

1. Is there anything that seems to be a nightmare in your life? If so, what is it?
2. How would you feel to know that you will awaken from the bad dream and it will have had no effect on you?
3. How have you received mercy, grace, or forgiveness in your life?
4. If you have been blessed so far, can you see how your blessing will only continue?
5. How might a big challenge be a sign that you are on the verge of a breakthrough?
6. Do you believe that pain or suffering buys you a place in heaven?
7. Would you be willing to trade in that old burdensome belief for a new belief that joy is your ticket to heaven?

Affirm:

No dark dream has power over me.

I awaken into the light of
my perfect wholeness.

Grace has always cared for me,
and it shall forever continue.

I replace any value in pain
with a value in total well-being.

17

Loved, Guided, and Sustained

Recently divorced Ivy Olson had two small boys, no money, and a nearly empty refrigerator as the holiday season approached. Depressed and fearful, she had no idea how she was going to care for herself and her family. Then an older woman in her garden apartment complex invited Ivy and her sons for Thanksgiving dinner. The neighbor laid out a feast of Ivy's favorite foods, and demonstrated she knew things about Ivy that she could not have known. The woman sent Ivy home with leftovers that would feed her family for a week. The unconditional love this neighbor showed Ivy gave her faith that she and her boys were going to make it through this tough time.

The next morning, Ivy went to the woman's apartment to return some Tupperware containers. Ivy looked in the window and was shocked to find the apartment completely empty, without a stitch of furniture. When Ivy went to the building manager to ask what had become of the woman, he told her that the apartment had been vacant for months. (YouTube: "Dinner with an Angel—It's a Miracle")

I am sustained by the love of God.

—W-50

We, too, are being guided and protected. Whether an angel whispers in your ear, or you have an uncanny intuition that proves itself, or the perfect person shows up at the right moment, you are being cared for by Higher Power. The same compassionate Source that blessed Ivy Olson and her boys is available to all of us. Love has no favorites and makes no exceptions.

In *A Course in Miracles*, Jesus makes it very clear that he and the grace of God are always with us. "'Who walks with me?' This question should be asked a thousand times a day, till certainty has ended doubting and established peace." (W-156.8:1-2) While the idea of separation takes many forms, the most fundamental one is that we are split off from the presence of God, and we are outside love's embrace.

Sometimes Spirit reaches us through direct inner guidance, and at other times through people and animals. My friend Peter, a musician in Philadelphia, had a terribly rough day. His girlfriend broke up with him, and when he went to his club engagement that night, his manager informed him that his band had been fired.

Utterly dejected, Peter began to make his way through the city streets. He grew so distraught that he set his guitar on the sidewalk, fell to his knees, and began to sob. At that moment a little stray puppy dog worked its way under Peter's arm and began to lick the tears off his cheeks. Peter felt so comforted by this miraculous intervention that he rose with renewed confidence and began to walk home, the puppy at his heels.

When Peter arrived, his girlfriend had returned, and she reported that his band manager had phoned to report that he had gotten the band an even better gig. Everything turned around in a short time. Peter invited his girlfriend to step onto the porch to meet the healing puppy, but it was gone. The little angel had done its job of teaching Peter that he was not alone, and the universe had his back.

> He will not leave you comfortless, nor fail to send His angels down to answer you in His Own Name.
>
> —S-2.III.7:5

Years ago, my girlfriend and I bought a house together. After several years, we decided to part amicably, and she would move out. The house was in a remote rural area, and when I considered the prospect of living there alone, I felt anxious. Part of me wanted to go out and find another girlfriend so I could avoid feeling lonely. But I decided not to give in to that temptation, and to instead consider being there alone as a spiritual opportunity.

To my happy surprise, I very much enjoyed my alone time. I did not need a girlfriend to save me from facing myself. I ended up using the time very productively. Eventually I entered another relationship, and when I did, I looked back with gratitude upon my decision to be with myself in a conscious way. When we recognize our identity as spiritual beings, we are never alone.

> You really think you are alone unless another body is with you.
>
> —W-76.3: 4

Space between relationships is highly empowering. I know people who jump from one relationship to the next with hardly any time in between. It's tempting after a breakup to lurch to find someone to fill your sense of emptiness. But the time after a breakup is a fertile opportunity to deepen your relationship with yourself. Many people lose themselves in a relationship, giving their power away to their partner, or becoming a satellite to their partner's world instead of retaining their own. If you chose a partner in order for that person to complete you, you overlooked the truth that you are already complete. Two half-people getting together does not add up to a whole person. Only when you bring fullness to a relationship can you enjoy your partner and yourself. "You recognize your brother as yourself, and thus do you perceive that you are whole." (W-159.2:3)

Many of us feel a sense of loss when someone dear to us passes on. While this is natural to our human experience, as divine beings we are not subject to loss. ". . . All loss comes only from your own misunderstanding. Loss of any kind is impossible." (T-8.VII.5:1-2) Many people experience profound connection and communication with loved ones who have passed on. We may even feel closer to them, since we are no longer separated by the illusion of physical distance. Our loved ones live vibrantly in our mind and heart, regardless of their physical absence. Medium Matt Fraser calls his seminars, "Love never dies." We might title a similar seminar, "Love is never alone."

In the movie *Heart and Souls*, little Thomas has five spirit guides constantly at his side. He talks with them and plays with them as normally as if they were human. His parents grow fearful of him cavorting with invisible friends, and tell him they are imaginary. Over time Thomas forgets about his spirit guides and goes on to a normal life. Yet they remain with him, though he sees them not.

As a man, Thomas hits a low point, immersed in emotional turmoil. Humbled, he asks for help, and his nonphysical friends reappear to him. We all have guides in spirit who are eager and ready to help us. But we must be open to receive their aid, and we must ask. "Then you will call, and the Lord will answer; you will cry for help, and he will say: Here am I." (Isaiah 58:9) You don't need to know who your guides are to receive their aid. You can simply call upon the Holy Spirit, Who will dispatch help in the most appropriate form.

You will be told exactly what God wills for you each time there is a choice to make.
—W-ep.5:3-4

The great Indian sage Ramana Maharshi's teachings run strikingly similar to *A Course in Miracles*. When the master was on his deathbed, his disciples sat beside him and cried, "Please, master, don't leave us!"

Sri Ramana smiled and replied, "Where could I go?"

The sage could make that statement because he knew his identity as Spirit, which dwells wherever anything lives. "God's Son cannot will death for himself because his Father is life, and His Son is like Him." (T-11.I.9:10) We can make that same statement with equal authority when we remember that the God Who created us lives within us, as us, through us.

We all have moments of aloneness, and we all have moments of deep connection with ourselves, each other, and God. *A Course in Miracles* is our impeccable guide to remember that aloneness does not exist in the mind of God, and therefore it does not exist in our right mind, or at all. A

Higher Hand holds ours, and when we reach to grasp it, we find all the comfort our heart desires.

> Whatever troubles you, be certain that He has the answer, and will gladly give it to you, if you simply turn to Him and ask it of Him. He will not withhold all answers that you need for anything that seems to trouble you. He knows the way to solve all problems, and resolve all doubts. His certainty is yours.
>
> —W-ep.1:5-8

Miraculous Insights:

1. Do you ever feel that you are alone? If so, how?
2. How might you be accompanied by helpers who are caring for you and protecting you?
3. Who are the physical angels in your life?
4. Who are the invisible angels in your life, helping you from the spiritual dimension?
5. Do you constantly need another person beside you, or can you remain peaceful and whole when you are seemingly alone?
6. Where do you think people go when they die?
7. How might your loved ones who have passed on remain with you?

Affirm:

I do not walk alone.

I am blessed with endless support in both the physical and nonphysical dimensions.

Everyone I have ever loved remains with me.

Love never dies.

18

Beautiful Dreamer

People who criticize you are making up stories in their mind about you. Usually the story is more about the critic than the recipient. Those who criticize you caustically don't know how to deal with their own feelings of inadequacy, so they attempt to relieve their distress by dumping their judgments on you. You can't afford to take angry criticism personally. It's not about you.

I attended a spiritual conference where a lecturer presented slides illustrating her lesson. One of the slides showed a drawing of a slot machine. As the lecturer went on to her next slide, a woman in the audience stood and shouted, "That proves it! You are an agent of the anti-Christ! Your last slide displayed '666'—the mark of the beast!"

Taken aback, the lecturer backed up to show the slide again, which depicted the slot machine with three cherries in its windows. It took a huge stretch of the imagination to interpret the cherries as "666"—but the woman who objected did exactly that. It was obvious to everyone in the audience that the intention was to present cherries, not numbers, and they laughed at the suggestion.

Here we have a very literal demonstration that the world is nothing more than a blank screen upon which we project our thoughts. ACIM proclaims, "There is no world! This is the central thought the course attempts to teach." (W-132.6:2-3)

If the world is a dream, then we are the dreamer. Nighttime dreams are unsubstantial because when we awaken, everything in the dream, pleasant or nightmare, dissolves. All of the characters that populated the dream, who seemed to be discreet entities separate from ourself, fade in the morning light. They were but figments of our imagination. What they seemed to be doing for us or against us, we were doing for or against ourself. They were not the cause of our experience. They represented our subconscious thoughts rising to the surface of our awareness so we can learn from them and, where necessary, heal them.

"There is no order of difficulty in miracles" (T-1.I.1:1) because there is no order of reality in illusions. We make up a story that one disease is harder to heal than another, or one childhood ordeal is especially difficult to overcome. Yet they are equally unreal dream diseases and dream ordeals. None of them have any power over us. The only real power is in our mind. Events are neutral. It is what we make of them that determines our experience. "I have given everything I see . . . all the meaning that it has for me." (W-2)

You can tell what is in your mind by what you are seeing on the screen of the world. If you are fixated on the Antichrist, you will find the Antichrist everywhere. If you are concentrating on the Christ, you will find the Christ wherever you look. The entire world is a huge inkblot test.

ACIM underscores the futility of trying to fix the world. We may be tempted to manipulate people or situations so they will conform to our desires and expectations. Yet if you have ever tried to fix your husband or wife, you know how frustrating and fruitless that is. I coached a woman who had just been released from the hospital after being treated for dangerously high blood pressure. The medication she was taking at home wasn't working.

"Is there some situation in your life by which you are feeling extremely pressured, or exerting extreme pressure?" I asked her.

"I feel frustrated trying to fix my husband," she answered.

"How long have you been trying to fix him?"

"Forty-two years."

"If you haven't fixed your husband in the past forty-two years, do you think you will be any more successful in the next forty-two years?"

"No," she admitted. "I'm starting to see that now."

Rather than attempting to change the environment, we need change the *in*vironment. "Therefore, seek not to change the world, but choose to change your mind about the world." (T-21.in.1:7)

Ramana Maharshi said, "A dreamer dreams that all the characters in his dream must awaken before he can." The dream characters do not need to awaken because they have no reality or volition of their own. They are the projections of the dreamer, not a condition for the dreamer's awakening. When the dreamer awakens, all the characters and events in the dream disappear. You cannot fix the world because it is not broken. It has no reality. Instead, we must heal our thoughts of brokenness.

> Perception is a result and not a cause.
>
> –T-21.in.1:8

I once led a week-long retreat in Portland, Oregon. One afternoon our group took a boat trip on the beautiful Willamette River. In preparation for the trip in a small open craft, I took my backpack with a bottle of water and I spread some sunscreen on my face and arms.

Just before the boat left the dock, I dipped my finger in the river to check its temperature. When I pulled my finger out of the water, I noticed it was covered with a thin film of oil. Immediately I grew irritated that this pristine river had become polluted from the motorboats that used it. "Maybe the oil is just from the boats at the dock," I tried to soothe myself.

A few minutes downstream, I poked my finger in the river again. To my dismay, the river still had an oil slick. Now I was really getting irked. "One of the last pure rivers in America is contaminated." I decided to try to be patient and wait until we were further downstream.

When we finally reached a remote portion of the river, I tested the water again. Tragically, the water was still polluted. My afternoon of delight had morphed to a depressing discovery.

Then I reached into my backpack to retrieve my water bottle, and I noticed my tube of sunscreen. Suddenly it dawned on me: The oil on my finger was not from the river. It was from my sunscreen. Because my finger was oily, whatever my finger touched seemed oily. The river was pure. My finger was polluted.

A polluted, sick, or evil world is the projection of polluted, sick, or evil thoughts. At first it may be distressing to realize that you are living in a dark story you made up. Yet this insight paves the pathway to freedom. If you authored an

> I am not the victim of the world I see.
>
> —W-31

oppressive story, you have the power to author a liberating story. If you don't like the plot, you can rewrite it. The best stories arc from a sinister plot to a rewarding conclusion. John Lennon said, "Everything will be okay in the end. If it's not okay, it's not the end."

A traveler in olden times came to the edge of a city, where he found a gatekeeper. "What's it like to live in this city?" he asked.

"What was it like where you came from?" the gatekeeper returned.

"It was an awful place. Crowded, crime, polluted, and lots of selfish people."

The gatekeeper shrugged his shoulders. "Well, that's pretty much what you'll find here."

The visitor shook his head and continued on his way.

An hour later another traveler approached the city gate. "What's it like in this city?" he asked the gatekeeper.

"What was it like where you lived?"

"A pretty nice place," the visitor replied. "Good people, safe, clean, easy to get around."

"Well, that's pretty much what you'll find here."

The visitor smiled and entered the city.

We keep finding the same results because we take our mind wherever we go. The one thing that all your problems have in common is your mind. Dr. Michael Ryce wrote a book entitled, *Why Is This Happening To Me . . . AGAIN?* He gives the example, "You fly away from New York to get away from a bad relationship, and the person who meets you at the airport in Los Angeles completes the sentence the person in New York began." The Law of Attraction continually draws to us people who play out our patterns of thinking. But that's not a bad thing. We keep facing the outpicturing of our hidden fear-based thoughts so we can heal them and get free.

A geographical or horizontal cure attempts to create a solution by manipulating logistics. A spiritual or vertical cure pierces to the causative level of mind. One is the story line; the other is the glory line. The story line is played out in the human drama. The glory line is the higher purpose of any experience that generates soul awakening. Most people attempt to improve the story line without addressing the glory line. Only inner transformation will take us where we need to go.

In an early *Star Trek* television episode, Captain Christopher Pike and a small crew visit a planet populated by mentally powerful beings. These aliens capture Pike and his crew, and exert a hypnotic effect on them so they believe they are in jail. After a while, Pike figures out that they are not really in jail, but they have fallen prey to the power of suggestion.

When the jailer brings the prisoners their meal, Pike wrestles him to the ground and begins to choke him. "You stop this illusion or I'll twist your head off!" he yells. Intimidated, the alien releases the spell, and the crew finds itself free in an open field.

The fall of Adam was the hypnosis into which we all entered when we dropped into the consciousness of the three-dimensional world and began to identify ourselves as physical bodies only. We believed we are separate from God and there is a world outside of us that generates our experience. *A Course in Miracles* urges us to break free of the belief that anyone or anything outside ourself causes our life. Renowned seer Edgar Cayce repeatedly stated, "Mind is the builder."

The world seems to be beset with many daunting troubles. Disease is rampant, the economy is volatile, and wars go on endlessly. The situations seem unique, but the story is nothing new. It's an old dream with the same characters in different costumes repeating the same lines, new wine in old wineskins that keep breaking. In the world, "it's always something." In Spirit, it's never anything. No illusion has more substance than another.

Jesus overcame the world by establishing himself in the glory line rather than staying stuck in the story line. You and I are called to achieve the same exalted state of mind. The Antichrist has no power over someone whose vision is founded in the Christ. The Antichrist is *invisible* to those who focus on Christ. Trying to purge the world of evil is as futile as the woman in that seminar audience yelling at the presenter who purportedly displayed "666." Instead, we must purge our mind of fearful thoughts. "Miracles are everyone's right, but purification is necessary first." (T-1.I.7:1) It is purification of our thoughts to which the Course refers.

The old film *Mighty Joe Young* tells of a huge King-Kong-like ape who is captured and wreaks havoc in a city. Then a pure-hearted woman quells his rampage by whistling the song, "Beautiful Dreamer." *A Course in Miracles* is whistling to us amidst a rampage of fear in the city of illusion, reminding us that we are all beautiful dreamers, using the mind that God has given us to create the story of our lives. The slide that seemed to show a threat to Christ is simply an innocent cartoon. We can toss aside any judgments, and recognize any attack on us, including our own, as the result of delusion. Then we can get on to the next slide in the show, unfettered by the projections of a fearful mind.

> You can indeed afford to laugh at fear thoughts, remembering that God goes with you wherever you go.
>
> —W-41.10:1

Miraculous Insights:

1. What stories have you made up about others being able to hurt you?
2. What better story of your safety and wholeness would you like to replace those old stories?
3. What old patterns or relationships do you see replicated in new situations or relationships?
4. What geographical cures (material manipulations) have you attempted that haven't worked?
5. What vertical cures (higher spiritual consciousness) might you apply that will work?
6. Walk around your room or outside your home and apply this statement to everything you see and do:

   "I am dreaming that I am seeing ...."

   or

   "I am dreaming that I am doing ...."

Affirm:

I trade old stories
that haven't served me,
for new stories that truly serve me.

I heal painful patterns
or relationships by applying
higher consciousness.

I awaken by recognizing that
I have been dreaming my life.

19

Heaven Can't Wait

A renowned samurai came to a Zen master and demanded, "Teach me about heaven and hell."

The master looked the warrior up and down, snickered, and replied, "Teach *you* about heaven and hell? You are an uneducated, thick-headed, arrogant buffoon. I wouldn't waste one moment trying to teach you about ideas you could never grasp."

Hearing that, the samurai grew furious. He began to breathe heavily, his cheeks reddened, and he lifted his sword to chop off the teacher's head.

Just as the warrior was about to strike, the master raised his hand and stated, "That, sir, is hell."

The samurai stopped and took a moment to absorb the teacher's statement. Suddenly he realized that the master was teaching him a profound lesson: We create our own hell by fear, anger, and unbridled emotions. Humbled, he bowed his head to the master's knee. "Thank you, sir, for a teaching that will change my life."

The master gently placed his hand on the samurai's shoulder, lifted his head, and found his eyes. "And that, sir, is heaven."

Heaven is not a place, but a state of consciousness. We do not have to wait to go to heaven or hell when we die; both states manifest in our lives now. Many of us have struggled through hell, and in flashes touched heaven, even as we walk the earth. Many religions teach that heaven is the afterlife reward for living a good life. Some teach that the more we suffer here, the more we earn paradise. Yet God does not dangle love like a carrot just beyond our reach. The heaven we hope for after death is available to us right where we stand.

> Why wait for heaven?
> It is here today.
> —W-131.6:1-2

I once flew into Newark airport on a hot summer Sunday evening. The place was crowded and noisy, and I felt put off. After a long trip, I just wanted to get home. My friend greeted me in the baggage claim area and began to lead me toward her car in the parking lot. Suddenly I realized I had made up a story about the airport that was keeping me from peace. Unhappy stories are our own creation. I invited my friend to sit with me for a moment, and I suggested, "Let's play a game called 'heaven.' Let's imagine that everything that is happening here is happening just as it is, but we are in heaven."

My friend was willing to play, so I went on.

"Look at those people coming through the arrival door," I pointed. "They have landed safely in heaven after a long trip away. They are greeting their loved ones with smiles, tears, and embraces. Their friends and relatives who arrived in heaven before them are welcoming them." I pointed toward the door that led to the street. "Limousines and tour guides await to show them to their destination."

My friend got into the game with me, and within a few minutes we were laughing and soaring. I no longer cared about getting home quickly. Already in heaven, where else would I need to go?

Consider all the things you have been told you must do or be before you can enter heaven: you have to lose 20 pounds; eat only organic food; master all the ACIM Workbook exercises; find your true soulmate; get rid of who you thought was your soulmate; go to church regularly; give lots to charity; trek through the Himalayas to sit at the feet of gurus; overcome your sexual fantasies; endure dinners with annoying relatives; vote evil politicians out of office; and on and on and on. Sheesh! No wonder so many people are tired and frustrated! Trying to earn heaven through an endless list of daunting tasks is exhausting!

A Course in Miracles cuts through all of those assumed prerequisites and assures us that we can enter heaven right now by opening to it and giving up our fascination with hell. The Workbook underscores, "Each time you practice, awareness is brought a little nearer at least; sometimes a thousand years or more are saved." (W-97.3:2-3) Talk about a time-saving device! We already stand where we are struggling to get. Ease is a far more powerful success tool than anxious striving. We can claim heaven now and beat the rush later.

In *Field of Dreams*, Ray Kinsella reunites with his estranged father, who asks his son, "Is this heaven?" When we drop our grievances and forgive ourselves and others, we are in heaven. Love *is* heaven.

Ray's dad tells him, "Heaven is where dreams come true." In the film, father and son connect on a ballfield in Iowa. But that setting is simply the stage on which heaven is played out. Heaven is not a geographical location; it is a reunion. "The holiest of all the spots on earth is where an ancient hatred has become a present love." (T-26.IX.6:1)

The Hawaiian spiritual tradition teaches that every newborn child is like a bowl of light. We love to be around children and pets because they are still connected to heaven and they radiate original innocence. They remind us who we are, where we come from, and where we are headed. Then, the Hawaiians teach, the world deposits rocks in the child's bowl. Fear, guilt, anger, resentment, and jealousy gradually displace the child's natural light until just a tiny trickle of the original luminescence shines through. By the time the child reaches adulthood, separation, pain, and sorrow overshadow the expression of divinity. *"This need not be."* (T-4.IV)

Healing does not require us to import anything we don't already have. It does not call us to any place other than where we are. Enlightenment is about peeling away what we are not, to reveal what we are. The Course is not about gaining love, but instead, "It does aim at removing the blocks to the awareness of love's presence, which is your natural inheritance." (T-in.1:8) When we let go of what is not heaven, only heaven remains.

ACIM tells us that the purpose of time is to learn to use it well. The ego, quick to usurp the Holy Spirit's intention, jumps in to co-opt time toward its own end, by placing well-being at some future date. But if it's not now, it's not. If it's not in heaven, it doesn't deserve to be here. The ego is all about wanting and waiting, not claiming and enjoying. "Its dictates, then, can be summed up simply as: "Seek and do *not* find." (T-12.IV.1:4) If you define yourself as a spiritual seeker, you will never find, because you are proceeding from a faulty premise. Define yourself as a spiritual finder, and you will be home everywhere, always.

An ancient fable tells that when the Earth had been formed and people were about to be placed on the planet, a group of gods got together and decided to set humanity on an adventure to find the secret of life. But where to hide it?

"Let's place the secret of life at the top of the highest mountain," one god suggested.

"No, people will be motivated to climb and they will find it easily," another replied.

"Then let's hide the secret at the bottom of the ocean," offered another.

"That won't work either. They'll invent submarines, and the game will be over."

The gods went round and round, trying to choose some physical location where human beings would not easily unearth the great secret.

Finally one god lit up. "I've got it!" he exclaimed. "Let's hide the secret of life inside each person. They'll *never* think to look there."

A Course in Miracles points us to look within for our answers. It urges us to quit searching the outer world, and take the deep dive. At every choice point, we will be brilliantly guided. The Course pierces beyond all of our attempts to place healing at a temporal or geographical distance. There is no time or space in heaven because it is everywhere always.

For I would follow You, certain that Your direction gives me peace.

—W-361-365

When we enter everywhere always through the portal of here and now, we are home. All the love we seek is right where we are. Knowing that, our hearts can soar with appreciation for the gifts with which we have been bestowed. And that, my dear samurai, is heaven.

Miraculous Insights:

1. How are heaven and hell not places you go after you die, but states of mind you experience while you live?
2. What hell have you created in your life?
3. What heaven have you created in your life?
4. How can you create less or no hell, and instead create more or all heaven?
5. Where have you sought the secret of life in the outer world? Have you found it there?
6. How might you seek and find the secret of life within yourself?
7. What do you think has to happen before you can be happy?
8. Could you choose happiness now, before anything else happens?
9. Take a situation in your life and turn it into heaven by applying more heavenly thoughts to it:

Affirm:

I turn hell into heaven
by choosing heavenly thoughts.

I do not have to wait
for anything to happen
before I can be happy

I choose total well-being now.

20

Your Divine Toolbox

My friend Brenda owns a successful restaurant in Seattle. She and her husband have worked hard for years to build its reputation and clientele. The couple has three children, ages 19, 17, and 15. Brenda confessed to me, "Soon all of our kids will be out of the nest. I'm afraid we've missed the best years of our lives, and theirs, because we were so focused on the restaurant while they were growing up. If we had to do it all over again, I would be with my family during those precious years, and build our business after they grew up."

The world gives us many tools to achieve success according to its standards. Yet it does not guide us to be successful spiritually. "If the only tool you have is a hammer, everything you see looks like a nail," said Abraham Maslow, known as the father of humanistic psychology. If your only tools are a body and an intellect, you will be able to navigate only the domain of bodies and intellects. Then you will gain the world, but miss your soul. A yogi described the physical dimension as "alluring, but ultimately unsatisfying."

A Course in Miracles provides a deep toolbox with many instruments to guide us home. But we have to put them into practice. A friend of mine bought a "reduce your belly" abdominal exercise machine. "How did that work for you?" I asked him.

"The damn thing didn't work . . .I threw it in the trash."

"How much did you use it?" I had to ask.

"Maybe five minutes a week."

Lots of people tell me that they started *A Course in Miracles*, but didn't know how to make it work in their lives. "Did you do the Workbook?" I ask. "No, I didn't get that far." Or, "I got to lesson 30, then put it aside." You can't blame a tool for not working if you don't use it. Twelve-step groups like Alcoholics Anonymous say, "the program works if you work it." So it is with ACIM. It will give back as much or as little as you invest in it.

I have often been prone to user error. I blame things for not working, when I did not operate them properly. Dee and I built a cottage in a remote area, which we powered with photovoltaic solar panels. When we returned after an extended absence, the PV system wasn't working. I grew upset with the engineer who installed the system and blamed him for faulty equipment or installation. When he came out to repair the product, he informed me that I did not keep sufficient water in the batteries. *Oops*. Easy to blame. Harder to take responsibility.

While some people complain that ACIM is too complicated, it is actually quite simple. There are really only two tools to choose from: the ego or the Holy Spirit; fear or love; illusion or truth. Each tool reinforces and takes us deeper into the thought system that upholds it. Ego hides in complexity. In the world, details

> This is a very simple course.
>
> —T-II.VIII.1:1

embellish. In Spirit, details distract. Nicholas Murray Butler, President of Columbia University, President of the Carnegie Endowment for International Peace, and a recipient of the Nobel Peace Prize, said, "An expert is someone who knows more and more about less and less until he knows absolutely everything about nothing." If you are going to become an expert at anything, let it be inner peace. ACIM teacher Michael Mirdad said, "Whenever you process the Course through the intellect rather than the heart, you crucify Christ all over again." We can understand *A Course in Miracles* somewhat through the mind, but that boat will take us just so far. It is not equipped to cross the ocean of *samsara*. Only the soul provides worthy transport.

Anthropologist Jane Goodall made the breakthrough discovery that chimpanzees, like human beings, make tools. She observed chimps taking a reed and poking it into a crevice in wood to dislodge termites the chimpanzees could eat. We might think of ACIM as a breakthrough tool to help us dislodge the termites of ego so they don't eat away the foundation of our life. If we want to be smart monkeys, we can practice this summary of *A Course in Miracles*: See no evil, hear no evil, speak no evil. In other words, "Do not see error." (S-2.I.3:3)

Any tool that reduces fear is worth using. In the documentary *(Dis)Honesty: The Truth About Lies*, a man recounts that he was on an airplane that encountered severe turbulence. A woman sitting near him was screaming, "We're going to crash and all of us will die!" The man told the woman that he was a structural engineer, and there was

All healing is essentially the release from fear.

—T-2.IV.1:7-8

no possible way the plane was going to crash. The woman calmed down considerably. The man was not a structural engineer at all, but his lie saved this woman emotionally, along with the other passengers her fright was spreading to. The man's lie was closer to the truth than her terrified mindset. The man employed a lighter illusion to offset a darker illusion, replacing a nightmare with a happier dream.

Tools are vehicles though which we give ourselves permission to be healed. While we may use prescription drugs, surgery, acupuncture, chiropractic, herbs, energy work, or prayer, the operative factor behind all of those tools is the mind. I often cite a brilliant passage from the Manual for Teachers: "Who is the physician? Only the mind of the patient himself. The outcome is what he decides that it is. Special agents seem to be ministering to him, yet they but give form to his own choice. He chooses them in order to bring tangible form to our desires. And it is this they do, and nothing else. They are not actually needed at all. The patient could merely rise up without their aid and say, 'I have no use for this.' There is no form of sickness that would not be cured at once." (M-5.II.2:5-13)

Our preferred tools work because we have faith in them. All healing is faith healing. A well-respected psychologist did a cross-cultural study of healing practices. He studied western medicine, Chinese medicine, spiritual healing, shamanism, voodoo, and other healing modalities. The study found that the results for all healing methods were the same: one-third of the patients improved, one-third remained the same, and one-third worsened. What better proof that healing or illness resides in the belief system of the patient more than the method?

If we're not careful, ego can get hold of our tool and wield it on its behalf. We think, "My tool is the best tool or the only tool, and everyone else's tool is inferior or wrong." But all tools work for some people, and we must respect their tool if it helps them. One night at a spiritual retreat I observed a woman reading *Emergency Magazine—True Stories of Ambulance Calls*. "How can you read such dramatic material just before bedtime?" I asked the woman. She smiled. "I work on the rescue squad, and this gives me some good ideas." That material would have given me nightmares, but it helped that woman sleep well.

> The outcome of the lesson that God's Son is guiltless is a world in which there is no fear, and everything is lit with hope and sparkles with a gentle friendliness.
>
> —T-31.I.8:1

Life has a purpose for everything. Even if we don't understand the purpose, it remains useful for those it can help. "I do not know what anything is for." (W-25) Humility calls us to accept the perfection of all creation. "We look on everyone as brother, and perceive all things as kindly and as good." (W-pII.14.3:4)

After a huge rainstorm, a river near my house deposited massive debris into the bay touching my favorite beach. The entire bay was covered with tree trunks and limbs as far as the eye could see. It was impossible to even get into the water, let alone swim in it. When I saw an ad in the local newspaper calling for volunteers to help clean up the debris, I went to join a community cleanup one Saturday morning.

After I and a hundred volunteers worked for several hours, we hardly made a dent in the mess. Even if we repeated the effort every week, it would take many months or even years to restore the beach. This was not a project that could be fixed piecemeal. It would take more than many hands to resolve the dilemma.

Then the county came in with heavy equipment. Excavators and bulldozers got the job done in a couple of days, and the beach was restored to its pristine nature. When we try to clean up the debris cluttering our mind piecemeal, we are in for a long, frustrating haul. Ego's attempts to fix ourself and the world ultimately fail. When we step back from futile egoic struggling and invite Holy Spirit to do for us what we cannot do for ourselves, it will bring in sophisticated equipment to do the heavy lifting and get the job done quickly, with no struggle on our part.

Ultimately, all tools are forms of magic, for we believe that something other than our mind is healing us. "Dismiss all foolish magical beliefs today, and hold your mind in silent readiness to hear the Voice that speaks the truth to you." (W-76.9:2) The Workbook and other spiritual methods are transitional tools, dreams that help us wake up. Yogis teach that if you have a thorn stuck in your foot, you can use another thorn to dislodge it. Then you can throw both thorns away. Eventually we must renounce all tools, including *A Course in Miracles*. "Forget this world, forget this course, and come with wholly empty hands unto your God." (W-189.7:5) Until then, we can be smart monkeys and use the instruments in our divine toolbox to take us home.

Miraculous Insights:

1. What tools has the outer world taught you that you need to achieve success? How well have they worked?

2. What spiritual tools do you use to gain inner peace? How well do they work for you?

3. How do the spiritual tools that work for you reflect your beliefs?

4. Can you allow other people to be successful with their tools, even if their beliefs do not match yours?

5. What project have you been laboring under, with little or no success?

6. Would you be willing to receive help from a Higher Power to accomplish your goal with no strain or struggle on your part?

7. Formulate your own prayer inviting Higher Power, by whatever name you know It, to step in and handle this project for you:

Affirm:

I am blessed with
spiritual tools that
make my life better.

I put my tools to good
and consistent use, and
I gain success and healing.

I give others the freedom
and support to use their tools,
even if they do not match mine.

21

Declare Your Independence

I used to date a woman who was a single mother of an unruly five-year-old boy. One day when she came to visit me with her son, he ran into the kitchen, grabbed a ripe banana from the counter, peeled it, and smashed it against a window, making a mucky mess. His mother laughed, thinking he was cute. When I asked her why she let him do that, she answered, "I want him to feel free."

Shortly afterward I had a coaching session with my mentor, an extraordinary spiritual guide. When I asked her opinion about the banana-throwing incident, she replied, "But he is not free to *not* throw the banana."

Most people equate freedom with the body. If I can do what I want, when I want, with my body, then I am free. *A Course in Miracles* takes a different view of freedom. It teaches that true freedom is freedom of the mind. "Do you want freedom of the body or of the mind? For both you cannot have. Which do you value?" (T-22.VI.1:1-3)

I used to visit a prisoner named Ray. When Ray was in college, he flew into a fit of rage and beat his girlfriend. Tragically, she died. Ray was convicted of manslaughter and sentenced to many years in prison. He used his time there for spiritual studies, including *A Course in Miracles*. He became a model prisoner and was given high-responsibility jobs. Ray was not a bad person; he had just made a terrible mistake. His heart was contrite. A few years before I met him, Ray became eligible for parole. But his girlfriend's parents, who were wealthy and politically influential, mounted an annual letter-writing campaign to "keep this vicious killer off the streets." Each time, he was denied parole.

As Ray told me his story, I realized that his body was restricted, but his soul was thriving. Meanwhile his girlfriend's parents had the physical amenities of royalty, but they were consumed with anger and revenge. Who was really in prison? Who was free?

People with physical challenges often find freedom in their mind. The beloved spiritual guide Ram Dass experienced a stroke, and he was largely confined to a wheelchair for the last years of his life. When I presented a program with Ram Dass, I played devil's advocate and asked him, "What would you say to someone who asks, 'How can I be happy when there is so much evil and suffering in the world?'" Ram Dass thought for a long moment, grew a quiet smile, and replied, "Change your mind."

Ram Dass's behavior was an even more compelling teacher than his words. In spite of his physical difficulties, he consistently maintained a light, joyful, loving attitude. He was amazingly happy, considering that his body was restricted. He demonstrated on a daily basis that the deepest freedom is of the spirit. Meanwhile many people dwell in perfectly healthy bodies, but they are miserable. Where does true freedom live?

While people with disabilities are often called "challenged," *A Course in Miracles* would not use that term. In the Manual for Teachers we are told, "There is no challenge to a teacher of God. Challenge implies doubt, and the trust on which God's teachers rest secure makes doubt impossible. Therefore they can only succeed." (M-4.II.2:5-7) Spirit cannot be challenged because there is nothing outside of wholeness, and no power greater than It. A teacher of God is not daunted, and soars above the appearance of challenge by observing all situations from a higher perspective. When the disciple Peter expressed doubt to Jesus, the master replied, "You are thinking as a man thinks, Peter. You must think as God thinks." (Matthew 16:23)

In Richard Bach's classic parable *Jonathan Livingston Seagull*, the mentor Chiang tells Jonathan, "To fly as fast as thought, to anywhere that is, you must begin by knowing that you have already arrived." Real travel is not of the body; it is of the mind. People or limiting circumstances may appear to control where your body goes, but no one can control where your mind goes. Dr. Stephen Hawking served as a striking teacher of the unbridled power of the mind. While his body was severely constricted, he was recognized as one of the most brilliant physicists of our age. His body could not stop his mind from probing the mysteries of the universe and shedding light on them.

Many people feel trapped because they do not have enough money. "If I had more money, I would be free," they think. Not really. If they just had more thoughts of freedom, they would be free. The Course affirms that we are abundant beings living in a universe that supplies us with all we need. If we feel poor, we have made up a story of lack and chosen to dwell in it. God has given us the power to create with our minds. We cannot create reality, which has already been created in utter opulence. But we can create our experience. The spiritual guide Bashar teaches, "You are always abundant in something. If you constantly think thoughts of lack, you are abundant in lack. You can just as easily become abundant in supply by focusing on thoughts of supply."

Other people feel trapped by their relationship. "If only I were single, I would have more freedom to do the things I want to do." Such a train of thought is a sure indication of specialness; you have given your partner undue power over your happiness. Here ACIM comes to the rescue with one of its most penetrating insights: "Only what *you* have not given can be lacking in any situation." (T-17.VII.4:1). Identify what you have been withholding, give it, and healing is sure to follow. We can't blame our partner for taking away our freedom. The thoughts we are choosing, not our partner, form the source of our experience of freedom or bondage.

Many people on the personal growth path cultivate the freedom "to just be myself." A most excellent pursuit! Yet we must decide which self we are free to be. If we seek freedom to be a body, ego, or personality, we will still not feel free, for we are bequeathing our identity to a finite, limited, death-prone self. If we seek freedom to be our divine Self, which is infinite, all-powerful, and eternal, we are onto real freedom.

> Let me not forget myself is nothing, but my Self is all.
>
> —W-358.I:7

We must allow others the freedom we wish for ourselves. To see another person as a body or personality only, keeps that person in prison. To see them as an unfettered spirit liberates them. To heal, we must release our friends from our belief that they are limited. When we recognize their invulnerable, immortal nature, we draw forth their authentic healed Self, and our own.

Many countries celebrate some form of Independence Day. Yet if we depend on liquor or drugs to make us happy, or our religion to be the only right one, or our partner to prove we are loveable, we are not independent at all. We are dependent on validation from the outer world, which sets us up for more emptiness and pain. Real independence is in-dependence, relying fully on the natural Self within. The God that created us loves us and walks with us always. "If you knew who walks beside you on the path that you have chosen, fear would be impossible." (T-18.III.3:2)

Thus we arrive at the most important freedom of all: freedom from fear and smallness. The only real liberation is soul liberation. When we peel away the illusions that breed unworthiness, victimization, and guilt, all that remains is love. Then we are free to be who God created us to be, the only freedom we ever sought, and the only one that matters.

Jesus spent a great deal of his ministry striving to liberate the Jewish people from guilt, burdensome rituals, and hypocrisy. Yet those same failings have worked their way into the religion that has grown up in his name. If you want to be a true Christian, walk in the same freedom from fear that Jesus demonstrated. Then you will fulfill his teaching to remember, "I am the light of the world. That is my only function. That is why I am here." (W-61.5:3-5) Jesus said that of himself, and now he says it of us. If you are wondering why you came to this world where night seems far longer than day, you have your answer.

Dr. Martin Luther King's gravestone is inscribed with one of his famous quotes: "Free at last, free at last, Thank God Almighty I'm Free at last." We don't have to die to get free. We just have to elevate our vision so we recognize our brother's wholeness, and our own. Only then can we say we are free, and *A Course in Miracles* has succeeded in creating the crucial shift in perception it came to deliver.

Miraculous Insights:

1. Do you feel free?
2. If not, where do you think greater freedom lives for you?
3. What freedom of the body do you seek?
4. What freedom of the mind do you seek?
5. Who do you know that has physical freedom, but is imprisoned mentally or emotionally? Why do you think they are trapped?
6. Who do you know that may have physical limitations, but is thriving spiritually? Why do you think they are thriving?
7. What does it mean to be "free at last?

Affirm:

I am free because I choose
thoughts of freedom.

No physical situation
can trap me.

I learn freedom from people
who are truly free.

I teach freedom of
the spirit by my example.

22

Beyond the Hero's Journey

Joseph Campbell was a brilliant mythologist who studied many of the world's religions, cultures, and fables, and found that they all told one story in common, which he called "The Hero's Journey." This universal plot is the archetype for drama as we know it. A person's regular life is interrupted by some challenge or encounter that calls him to a greater adventure. He must solve a problem or defeat a foe in order to save himself or a loved one, or fulfill a vision. Along the way he is confronted by foes who threaten him, and he joins with allies who aid him. Eventually he must do battle with the evil nemesis, representing his greatest fear. When he conquers the demon, he wins the holy grail, symbolizing spiritual enlightenment. Then the hero returns to the community and shares the gift he has obtained, for the betterment of all.

On a practical level, *A Course in Miracles* is very much in accord with the hero's journey. We begin to awaken to the fact that the life we have been living is shallow, meaningless, or misdirected. This motivates us to set off on a quest to discover who we are and understand our purpose for living.

Along the way we must face our inner fear-based demons, and conquer them by choosing love instead. Many of the Workbook lessons urge us to confront fear and overcome it. When we do, we gain the capacity to help others. Course author Jesus Christ depicts himself as one who has completed the journey we all share, and he lingers a while to take our hand and guide us to the heaven in which he is established, our true home.

Yet *A Course in Miracles* would take us beyond the hero's journey. At the highest level of its teaching, there are two elements of the hero's journey to which the Course takes exception: "hero" and "journey."

ACIM mentions the word "hero" seven times, all describing the ego's self-cast role as the center of the universe. Jesus devotes an entire section of the Text to illuminating and dismantling "The Hero of the Dream." The ego believes that the world revolves around it, and life's purpose is to maintain the ego's safety and fulfill its desires, primarily of the body. Everyone and everything that enables the ego's triumph is a friend, and everyone and everything that opposes it is enemy. The world is in the mess it is in because everyone is championing his or her own hero self, with separate interests. God help anyone who gets in the way of the "hero's" victory.

One day while I was driving along a country road, I approached a woman walking her two small dogs off-leash. Being a dog lover, I slowed down to minimum speed and steered far clear of the woman and her pets. But that was not good enough for her. She shook her fist and yelled, "You should drive on another road!" As the hero of her dream, the purpose of the road was for her to walk her dogs, and anything that threatened that was not allowed. As hero of my dream, the purpose of the road was a thoroughfare for me to drive to my destination. Behold two incompatible dreams—the story of the world, which multiplies separate heroes times billions.

The "hero" plot runs far beyond individual personalities. We project hero identities onto celebrities, gurus, sports teams, corporations, religions, and nations, to name a few. Most religions believe that their way to God is the only way, and everyone else is going to hell. The world rotates around their chosen savior, and all others are deluded or irrelevant. A rabbi at my Jewish college taught, "The history of Israel is the history of the world." Yet he failed to consider that lots of significant events have occurred in the world that had nothing to do with Israel. Billions of people have lived and died who never heard of Israel, and whose lives were not affected by it in the least. But if you are Jewish and you value Israel, that history, land, and religion colors your entire world.

Christians believe that anyone who has not taken Jesus Christ as their personal savior is doomed to hell. Yet many people have become very close to God, even one with God, and they do not relate to Jesus as savior. The word "Christ" means "illuminated." Lots of souls have found their way to God and their Christed nature outside of Christianity. The true Christ spans far beyond the religion that grew up in his name. But if Christianity is the hero of your dream, all else is error.

Nationalism is a massive hero dream. Countries go to war over ideologies, real estate, and oil rights. Members of one gender believe they are superior to the other. Mac users and PC afficionados put each other down. Politicians vote along party lines regardless of what their conscience tells them. Some parents smash each other with beach chairs at little league baseball games. And on and on and on. The history of the world is not the history of Israel or Jesus. It is the history of the hero's dream.

While the hero's dream is utterly in vain, the Holy Spirit offers us a blessed substitute. We can upgrade our hero's journey by shifting from a "What can I get?" quest to a "How can I help?" mission. Even if you are living in an illusion, you can make it an illusion of soul reward. Instead of being a hero just to yourself, you can be a hero to the world. When you look for ways to relieve the suffering of others, you relieve your own suffering. Rescue a dog or cat. Volunteer as a big brother or big sister. Write an uplifting book, movie, or piece of music. Sing, dance, or teach. Inspire others with your painting. Invent something that will make many lives easier. The Holy Spirit can take the ego's goals and turn them into a divine quest. You will not end the tyranny of ego by fighting it, but by repurposing it as an instrument of Higher Power. Spiritual masters train their egos to do God's will. *Maya* usually doesn't dissolve overnight; enlightenment often occurs in stages. We continually trade heavier dreams for lighter ones. Then we walk off the stage instead of leaping from it.

Just as the Course transcends the idea of "hero," it sheds new light on the idea of "journey." The journey we seem to be on exists only within the dream of the world. In reality, we never went anywhere. There is no

> The journey to God is merely the reawakening of the knowledge of where you are always, and what you are forever. It is a journey without distance to a goal that has never changed.
>
> –T-8.VI.9:6-7

place to go because the real you has never left heaven. Even while you walk through the dream of the world, your true self remains eternally established in Spirit. Ego travels and evolves. Spirit can never become anything but what It is, and It remains forever. "Enlightenment is but a recognition, not a change at all." (W-188.1:4)

There is one more significant difference between Joseph Campbell's Hero's Journey and the Course's. Campbell's version depicts the Hero's Journey as ever continuing. You don't just take the ride, claim the chalice, deliver your gift to the community, and you are done. When you have mastered one level of life, you are called to a new level of the journey to master. Campbell maps the journey, but never folds up the paper on which it is inscribed.

Through the progression of Campbell's journey, we rise to higher and higher levels of illumination and work our way off the karmic wheel. In a way, it is so. Jesus and other spiritual masters graduated from the school of Earth we all attend. They show the way out, so we may follow their lead and enjoy the freedom they found. Yet there is a paradox in this paradigm: *The way out is to recognize that you were never in.* Your divine self was never trapped in a body. You were free all the while, but you just didn't know it. You can get out anytime you wish. But your intention to escape has to be stronger than the attraction to stay. ACIM bolsters that higher intention. The life God has in store for us far exceeds the one we have been living. Why would you stay in prison when you hold the key to freedom in your hand?

In the movie *The Truman Show*, Truman Burbank has unknowingly lived his entire life on a massive television set where the producers contrive and control his every interaction. Eventually Truman begins to suspect that his world is fake, and he seeks an avenue of escape. Meanwhile a reporter interviews Christof, the diabolical director who programs Truman's encounters. The reporter asks Christof, "Can Truman escape?"

Christof answers, "He can leave at any time . . . Ultimately, Truman prefers his cell."

While the ego prefers its cell, Spirit knows there is more. That is the impetus for the Hero's Journey. But when we arrive in heaven, we discover we never left. Only in dreams do we trade a darker existence for a lighter one. In reality, we carried paradise within us all the while. The fall of Adam was not physical; it was psychic. God did not kick Adam and Eve out of the Garden of Eden. They chose to leave by eating from the tree of good and evil, stepping into a mindset of dualistic separation rather then perfect inherent unity. We re-enter the Garden by remembering the wholeness that exists behind the appearance of opposing forms. In heaven there are no opposites. Light and dark, good and evil, life and death do not rotate or vie for dominion. Only light, good, and life exist. This is a difficult concept for the ego to grasp because its very existence depends on the juxtaposition of opposites and ongoing conflict. Yet there is a dimension beyond opposites which represents the hero's final awakening.

Worthwhile belief systems contain a graduation mechanism. They do not define you as stuck in one identity or reality for your entire life or forever. There is a reality beyond the Hero's Journey. You are not required to battle evil for eternity. Leave that to *Star Wars*. On the other side of the Hero's Journey is the Hero's Arrival. The real Hero's Journey works its way out of the journey altogether.

Joseph Campbell's brilliant contribution to help us understand our worldly walk is paramount. To bottom line the dynamics of the human drama is no small task. But he achieved it. ACIM goes a step farther and reveals to us that we are greater than any drama we perceive. "The senselessness of conquest is quite apparent from the quiet sphere above the battleground." (T-23.IV.9:5) The events of the world cannot touch the Son of God, the identity we all share. Every moment of the human journey is designed to lead us to our divinity. Then we can put all journeys behind us and celebrate our glorious homecoming.

Miraculous Insights:

1. What Hero's Journey are you on?
2. How have you progressed on your Hero's Journey?
3. What does it mean to be "the hero of the dream?"
4. Do you believe the Hero's Journey goes on endlessly, or is there a conclusion?
5. How do you successfully complete your Hero's Journey?

Affirm:

I am on a spiritual journey
that leads beyond all journeys.

I master the lessons before me
and I claim my identity
as a whole, perfect soul.

23

Hastening the Last Judgment

After I moved into a new home in a well-manicured neighborhood, I discovered down the road a large empty lot strewn with junk cars, rusty trucks, and unsightly trash. I grew distraught as I foresaw guests coming to my home passing this ugly scene, and I resented the lot's owner for messing up the neighborhood.

A few days later, the shipping container holding my family's possessions from our previous home arrived at the local port. When I hired a trucker to deliver the container, he informed me that the 45-foot container would not be able to negotiate a sharp turn into our subdivision. The trucker suggested, "Why don't you ask the guy who owns the empty lot on the corner if you can park the container there while you unload it?"

Suddenly the empty lot became attractive. I phoned the owner, who was quite congenial and told me, "Sure, no problem." We had the container delivered there, and kept it on the site for a few days until we completed unloading.

Now I see how hasty and shortsighted were my judgments about the lot and the owner. When he agreed to help me, the lot became a gift rather than a problem, and the owner a good neighbor. Now when I pass the lot, I have pleasant and grateful memories of it.

> And in His judgment will a world unfold in perfect innocence before your eyes.
>
> —W-164.5:4

A judgment is one snapshot of a person or situation in one moment from one angle. But there are other angles that reveal very different facets. When we achieve a shift in perception, the bad becomes good, the enemy a friend, and the empty full.

While visiting a petting zoo, I observed a customer at the snack bar making a loud, nasty scene because he didn't like the service. As I watched the incident, I made a mental note to avoid the unruly man.

A few minutes later, as I was passing the deer enclosure, I saw the back of a man kneeling to feed a deer. As the fellow kindly, sweetly stroked the deer's face, he reminded me of St. Francis. Then the man turned his head and I saw that this saintly soul was the very devil who had caused the big ruckus at the snack bar! My view of him with the deer fulfilled the prayer of ACIM Workbook Lesson 161, "Give me your blessing, holy son of God." (W-161)

We've all practiced judgment for much of our lives. We were taught at a tender age to like this and hate that, approve or reject the people our parents indicated, and we inherited their gender, ethnic, racial, religious, political, and cultural prejudices. We also learned terrible judgments about ourselves. "You're too fat." "Why don't you get better grades like your elder sister?" "If you don't go into the family profession, you'll be a failure and we will be embarrassed." "Don't cry, son, people will think you are a sissy." "No one will marry you past a certain age." And on and on and on and on. It's a wonder that we continued to get up each morning and trudge through our days, carrying such a load of burdensome beliefs!

Fortunately, the Holy Spirit has an answer to the world of judgment. ACIM tells us plainly, "God did not create a meaningless world." (W-14) The world of judgment is not God's world. It is a sick story the ego made up, fabricated with fear. The Holy Spirit has another story:

> Spirit am I, a holy Son of God,
> free of all limits, safe and healed and whole,
> free to forgive, and free to save the world.
>
> —W-97.7:2

Rumi described freedom from judgment in this way: *"Out beyond ideas of wrongdoing and rightdoing, there is a field. I'll meet you there."* It is to this field that *A Course in Miracles* invites us. But we must be vigilant to plant ourselves firmly in the field. It is tempting to drop back into fear, doubt, and criticism. For that reason, Rumi urges us three times in the same poem, *"Don't go back to sleep."*

One of my favorite passages is the Workbook section, "What is the Last Judgment?" (W-pII.10) While religions have instilled humanity with tremendous fear of the Last Judgment, loaded with horrible visions of eternal hell in its grisly aftermath, ACIM explains that the Last Judgment is simply the last time we judge. Hallelujah! Pits of fire do not await on the other side; judgment *is* the pit of fire. Judgment is self-punishing the moment we indulge in it. The Last Judgement is the crucial turning point when hell gives way to heaven. Thus we have every reason to look forward to the Last Judgment, and do everything we can to hasten it.

The Course underscores the impotence of judgment by describing a kind of cosmic court case in which you stand before the Creator, cowering as you await a verdict punishing you for your sins. Yet, "You need not fear the Higher Court will condemn you. It will merely dismiss the case against you. There can be no case against a child of God . . . Appeal everything you believe gladly to God's Own Higher Court . . . because [the Holy Spirit] speaks for Him and therefore speaks truly. It will dismiss the case against you." (T-5.VI.10:1-5)

While my friend Tom was passing his college bookstore, he saw a display of recently-published yearbooks outside the front door. He had no money, so he grabbed a book and stole it. Over the next few days Tom felt guilty, so he returned the book to the store and confessed to the manager that he had stolen it. The manager smiled and directed him to a sign beside the display that Tom had not seen: Free—Please Take One.

In like manner, we believe we have stolen our good from a universe that, in contrast to the ego's dark rantings, is happy to provide us with everything we need for free. Burdensome earning is a story the ego made up. The deceiver tells us that unless we are sweating and struggling to wrest our good from the hands of a stingy, reluctant universe, we don't deserve it. If our life is easy or happy, we may judge ourselves as lazy or selfish, and feel guilty. But God wants us to have all of our good not because of what we do, but because of who we are. Jesus asked, "If imperfect parents know how to lovingly take care of their children and give them what they need, how much more will your perfect heavenly Father give the Holy Spirit's fullness when His children ask him?" (Luke 11:13)

I once asked Ram Dass if it is spiritually acceptable to pray for a specific result. He answered, "If you could know all the ramifications of that result in your life, and in the lives of everyone you touch, yes. But you cannot know for sure how any act will ultimately affect your life and the world." This is the reason we cannot judge. You never know how anything you do, including your sins or errors, fits into the grander scheme of your life and the universe. Sometimes our darkest deeds lead to the brightest light.

I met a man named Tony who was a disciple of the apparitions at Medjugorje, Croatia. Beginning in 1981, Mother Mary miraculously appeared to six teenagers in that remote village, and gave them blessings, instructions, and messages for the world. Tony took upon himself the ministry of showing films about those sacred events, passing along the messages.

After I attended Tony's presentation, I asked him how he got into this unique ministry. "I wasn't always interested in spirituality," he explained. "I used to be very shy and introverted. I hated doing anything that required me to stand in front of a group. But I did like to tell dirty jokes, which got me attention. I developed a reputation as an off-color comedian, and I got stand-up gigs. I gained a great deal of confidence in my ability to speak before a crowd.

"When I learned about the Medjugorje miracles, I experienced a spiritual conversion. I was so touched that I wanted to share this inspiring message. I lost interest in my comedy and began to speak and teach on the miracles. Now I realize that my raunchy career was a preparation for me to step into this ministry."

The Book of Genesis tells how Joseph's jealous brothers cast him in a pit and left him to die. Then a miraculous series of events propelled Joseph to the position of Governor of Egypt. When a famine fell over Israel, Joseph's brothers had to go to Egypt to beg for food. There they were directed to none other than Joseph. When they pleaded for forgiveness for attempting to kill him, Joseph answered, "You meant it for evil, but God meant it for good." (Genesis 50:20)

> Now are we saved indeed. For in God's Hands we rest untroubled, sure that only good can come to us.
>
> —W-194.9:1-2

The ego sees wrongdoing, while the Holy Spirt sees innocence. Here again we do well to remember the instruction, "Do not see error." (S-2.I.3:3) If you are seeing error, you are in ego. If you are seeing perfection, you are in Spirit. "All things work together for good. There are no exceptions except in the ego's judgment." (T-4.V.1:1-2)

We may not get over judgment overnight. The ego is astonishingly crafty at defending its soulless empire. It hurls endless tricks to reinforce belief in separation. We can begin to dethrone the insane despot by noticing when we are judging, and recognize how awful it feels. When I find myself judging, I ask myself as quickly as possible, "Is there another way to look at this that would make me feel more peaceful?" There always is. Then I experience the blessed homecoming of the prodigal son. "If nothing but the truth exists, right-minded seeing cannot see anything but perfection." (T-3.II.3:5)

Like Rumi, ACIM goes beyond our judgments of right and wrong, good and bad. Judging something as good is also a judgment we need to transcend. The Mind of God spans far beyond our human ideas of what is right and what a good person should do. The light of heaven does not need darkness as contrast; true life knows no death. There is a deeper meaning to Lesson 268, "Let all things be exactly as they are." On one level, the lesson calls us to let the world be what it is. On a deeper level, we are asked to recognize that love is the only reality, and we need to let love be all there is.

The ego's world is built on judgment. Spirit's world is based on releasing judgment. Contrary to what many religions have told us, there is no judgment in heaven. Heaven, in fact, is the absence of judgment. Can you imagine a day, week, or life without judgment? Or even an hour? Or a minute? Suspending judgment, for any length of time, is the best thing that could happen to each of us and the world. If you must think about the Last Judgment, pray that it come soon, for it is the doorway to life.

> You who believed that God's Last Judgment would condemn the world to hell along with you, accept this holy truth: God's Judgment is the gift of the Correction He bestowed on all your errors, freeing you from them, and all effects they ever seemed to have.
>
> —W-pII.10.3:1

Miraculous Insights:

1. Who are you holding some judgment against?

2. How might your judgment be based on a particular version of that person, seen from one perspective at one moment?

3. How might you see a more congenial version of that person from a different perspective?

4. How might you call that person "friend?"

5. How might something you consider your "sin" be just a big nothingburger?

6. How might something bad that happened to you turn out to be something really good?

Affirm:

I release judgment
in favor of healing.

As I change my mind
about the world I see,
the world I see changes.

I choose innocence
for myself and everyone.

My soul is at peace.

24

We All Go Home Together

An ancient Hindu fable tells of a spiritual seeker who hears there is a portal to heaven at the top of the Himalayas. So he sets out on the arduous trek with his loyal dog at his side. Together the two traverse daunting terrain, ford angry rivers, and push through heavy snowstorms. Finally they arrive at the summit of a high mountain, where the sacred portal opens. A brilliant light pierces the clouds and an angel appears, who informs the aspirant that he can now enter heaven—but he will have to leave his dog behind. The man thinks for a short moment and tells the angel, "If my dog cannot get into heaven with me, I am not going." At that moment the dog transforms and reveals his true identity as Krishna, and the two enter paradise together.

The story is a metaphor for the journey to God we all share. We can substitute any valued person or pet for the role of the dog in the story. Why would you want to get into a heaven that would not welcome those you love? (Personally, I would be very wary of any heaven that did not accept dogs, who bring heaven to earth for humans.)

> There is no obstacle that you can place before our union, for in your holy relationship I am there already. We will surmount all obstacles together, for we stand within the gates and not outside. How easily the gates are opened from within, to let peace through to bless the tired world!
>
> IV-B.5:3-5

The ego's constant question is, "What's in it for me?" Spirit's question is, "How can it work for all of us?" Partners of narcissistic people complain that their mate's motto is, "It's all about me." Yet I saw a bumper sticker: It's all about we.

One of my friends was in a Tokyo subway car when the city's electricity failed after the massive 2011 earthquake. When the passengers realized the electricity was not going to be restored quickly, they calmly exited the train car and found their way to a ladder to the street. There they all helped each other ascend to safety. No one panicked and no one ran ahead of the group. Their motto was, "We're all in this together, so let's cooperate to get everyone free."

That scene is reminiscent of the January 2009 day when an airplane was forced to make an emergency landing in New York's Hudson River. When boat captains on the river observed the plane's dilemma, they guided their vessels to the site and made themselves available to rescue passengers. Meanwhile, pilot Chesley "Sully" Sullenberger stayed with the aircraft and patrolled the cabin until he was sure that all the passengers and crew had exited

> Your mind will elect to join with mine, and together we are invincible.
>
> —T-4.IV.11:5

safely. He assumed responsibility for the well-being of everyone on his aircraft.

Then there was the moment in Kazakhstan when a dog fell down a steep concrete embankment and got caught on the edge of a raging canal. If the dog slipped or the canal rose, the creature would have surely been swept to its death. A passerby had compassion for the dog's dilemma and slid down the slope to help. On the bank above, six men gathered and held hands to form a human chain to descend the steep embankment until they were able to grasp the frightened pooch and pass it up to safety. (YouTube: "Most Intense Human Chain Ever Rescues Dog Stranded in Canal")

> What we can accomplish together has no limits, because the Call for God is the Call to the unlimited.
>
> —T-5.II.12:5

A Course in Miracles underscores that all healing is shared. The Course tells us many times that joining is the will of God, and yields far more powerful results than pursuing separate interests. Only the ego believes that good is given to one at the expense of another.

For many years I have been practicing the motto, "There is no private good." If something is truly good for you, it will bless others as well. On a hot Seattle afternoon Dee and I went into a restaurant, where the hostess seated us beneath the duct of an air conditioning unit that blew cold air on us. After a while we were quite chilly. We wanted to ask the waiter to reseat us, but we had already been served our appetizer, and I felt guilty about bothering the waiter. But eventually we decided to trust our instinct, and the waiter kindly reseated us several tables away from the duct.

A few minutes later, the hostess seated an elderly couple at the table we had vacated. As soon as they sat down, the man smiled and issued a long sigh of relief. "Ah, cool air—just what I needed," he said with a smile. "Brother, we heal together as we live together and love together." (T-11.VIII.11:4)

One of the most famous affirmations of oneness came in 1914 during World War I. As Christmas approached, British and German troops had been bitterly battling for five months. In honor of the holiday, armies decided to call off the war for a day and celebrate together. Over 100,000 soldiers from both sides got together, shared dinner, gave each other gifts, took photographs with one another, and some played football in the land between the two sides. What an inspiring demonstration that we can choose peace when we hold that intention!

> You and your brother will yet come together in my name, and your sanity will be restored.
>
> —T-4.IV.II:6-7

> Alone we can do nothing, but together our minds fuse into something whose power is far beyond the power of its separate parts. By not being separate, the Mind of God is established in ours and as ours. This Mind is invincible because it is undivided.
>
> —T-8.V.1:6-8

Agreement is powerful. Because every thought is creative, whatever we agree on becomes true in our experience. "Where two or more are gathered in My Name, there am I with them." (Matthew 18:20) We can gather in the name of love, or in the name of fear. The crazy world seems real only because lots of people believe in it. When we withdraw our belief in illusions, only truth remains. "Brother, you need forgiveness of your brother, for you will share in madness or in Heaven together." (T-19.IV-D.12:7)

To the ego, bodies being together constitutes unity. But we have all had the experience of being with someone physically, while feeling separate spiritually. Nothing is lonelier than physical proximity coupled with spiritual absence. You can be lying next to someone in bed, but you feel worlds apart. (The Japanese say, "same bed, different dreams.") By contrast, you can have a dear friend or family member who lives thousands of miles away, and whom you see rarely, but when you think about them, you feel totally connected. When you meet after a long time, you feel as if you have never been apart. "One instant spent together with your brother restores the universe to both of you." (T-18.VII.5:3-4)

> And so they wander through a world of strangers, unlike themselves, living with their bodies perhaps under a common roof that shelters neither; in the same room and yet a world apart.
>
> –T-22.in.2:8

While we believe we are separate from God, each other, and ourselves, it is not so. Unity is truth, division illusion. We do not need to do anything to make oneness happen. We just need to drop the belief that we are isolated. I saw a photo of a couple sitting on a couch beside one another, each wearing a virtual reality headset. Each person was completely immersed in a reality divorced from the other. This is the story of many relationships and the world. We are all walking around wearing a VR headset, watching our own distinct movie.

Yet the moment comes when we tire of the fragmented movie, and we decide, "There has to be more." So we courageously remove our blinders and discover a reality that far transcends the tiny mad idea the ego conjured. In that expanded world we find each other. I know a number of people who, through DNA testing, have found their birth mother after being adopted, or connected with valued relatives they have never met. In many cases they report that their sense of reunion and homecoming is life-changing. My friend Charlene's mother had become pregnant as a teenager; she never told the father he had a child, and gave the baby up for adoption. When Charlene, at the age of 35, finally found her father, his family threw her a welcoming party. When Charlene entered the room, she was greeted by a huge "It's a Girl!" sign.

We are all destined for a momentous homecoming that far transcends Charlene's. We are certain to one day remember who we are, where we came from, and where we are headed. We will drop our false identity as separated, bereft, sinful souls, and reclaim our true identity as innocent, loveable, divine beings. That day is closer than you think. Shall we let it be today?

> You and your brother are coming home together, after a long and meaningless journey that you undertook apart, and that led nowhere. You have found your brother, and you will light each other's way. And from this light will the Great Rays extend back into darkness and forward unto God, to shine away the past and so make room for His eternal Presence, in which everything is radiant in the light.
>
> —T-18.III.8:5-7

Miraculous Insights:

1. Is heaven exclusive for people who think like you do, or does everyone have a right to enter heaven?

2. Would you not enter heaven if you had to leave someone you love behind?

3. What challenging situations have you overcome because you joined with one or more other persons and made a team effort?

4. How would you be living your life differently if you knew you were never separate from God, you carry God with you, and the love of God always surrounds and supports you?

Affirm:

God lives in me, through
me, with me, and for me.

I deserve heaven,
as do all the children of God.

I delight in joining with others
to achieve our valued goals.

I am one with the family of Spirit.

Epilogue

We can all use a miracle. You might yearn to receive an answer to a prayer, heal from a disease, resolve a painful relationship, or find money to pay your bills. Or you might long to re-ignite your waned passion or find your right place in the great scheme of all things. From where you are standing, you don't see how that could happen. You may have tried and tried, prayed and prayed, practiced and practiced, and not yet seen a result. You believe it would take an act of divine intervention for your prayer to be answered.

I am here to tell you that such divine intervention is absolutely available. You are not lost, abandoned, or outside love's embrace. Your prayer will be answered with a miracle, a shift in perception from fear to love, often followed with a material manifestation. Your vision will be cleansed, you will find the pathway home, and you will walk it. While you are seeking a physical result, you are secretly being trained in spiritual awakening.

God does not want you to experience a miracle and then go back to a life devoid of true joy. God wants miracles to become a way of life for you. Then, instead of going from one grueling task to another, your days will become a string of blessings, each one outdoing the last one.

If this vision seems outlandish to you, you can see how far you have drifted from your natural state of knowing your deep worthiness. Yet despair not. There is always a turning point. The prodigal son realizes that eating the pigs' slop is not how he was born to live. He turns about and sets foot on the path toward his father's home that he left in haste. Now he wants the safety and security of his homeland more than the glitter the far country dangled before him.

If you have completed reading *Of Course in Miracles*, you are on the homecoming trajectory. You have made a choice for healing. You are headed in the right direction. You have the wisdom, tools, and vision to cross the finish line.

As *A Course in Miracles* tells us many times, you do not walk alone. Legions of unseen helpers are cheering for you and championing your cause. Take hope and take faith. You are more deeply loved than you have ever imagined. Those who have walked by your side will stay with you. The hand of grace that has taken you this far will not stop now.

Even while your ship cuts through the sea in the dark of night, you can see the lights of the city of refuge on the shore. You will reach the safe harbor and once again walk on solid ground. God keeps His promises. As God's child, you will keep yours. Only the veils of illusion make it seem as if the vows of Spirit can be broken.

I don't simply wish you miracles. I *see* them for you. I *know* your divine right to them. The time will come when we look back on our earthly journey, have a good laugh, and wonder, "What was I thinking?" But now we think anew. We use the mind that God gave us to empower ourselves and each other. Then miracles will fill our days as fully as hardship once did. If you can believe even for a moment that you deserve all the gifts your heart desires, you open the door for them. The treasure house you find them in will be far vaster than any treasure troves you sought on earth.

Thank you for sharing this journey with me. We walk hand in hand to the mountaintop, none left behind. There we will plant the flag of victory, and claim earth in the name of heaven.

Acknowledgments

I hereby acknowledge the God of All That Is as the Center and Source of my life, and all the blessings that come to me and the entire world.

His beloved Son Jesus Christ, the author of *A Course in Miracles*, lives as a shining gift to me and all humanity, and identifies all of us as equal Children of God. Delivering that sacred text to humanity is an act of grace and compassion that goes far beyond anything the Intellect could conjure or understand.

As always, my deep gratitude to my beloved partner Dee, who practices *A Course in Miracles* with me, and supports me to live its teachings and share them. We talk about things that matter to our souls, and empower our relationship as a home for miracles.

This has been another rewarding opportunity for me to work with some extraordinarily talented professionals. Elena Karoumpali of L1graphics has turned out a stunning cover, complemented by Isabel Robalo of IsaDesign's very tasteful and artistic interior design. Alyssa Freeland has been a huge help with her impeccable and thoughtful proofreading.

Profound thanks to Dr. Helen Schucman for bringing the Course to the world, in spite of her fierce resistance.

Dr. Bill Thetford kept encouraging Helen to persevere, and his kind heart made him a model Teacher of God.

Dr. Kenneth Wapnick devoted himself to editing the Course for publication, and then proliferating its wisdom by applying his penetrating understanding of its principles.

Humble gratitude to Judith Skutch Whitson for working diligently to publish ACIM, and make it available to all of us in an easily accessible form. Her husband at the time, Robert Skutch, contributed immensely to that process, followed with his book, *Journey without Distance*.

Reed Erickson is little known by most Course students, but deserves major kudos for donating the funds for the first edition of *A Course in Miracles*.

Dr. Jerry Jampolsky served on the early board of the Foundation for Inner Peace, and helped popularize ACIM with his concise book, *Love is Letting Go of Fear*. Marianne Williamson furthered that effort in a big way, with the support of Oprah Winfrey.

Dr. Jon Mundy and Carol Howe were students of the Course from its inception, and they have devoted their lives and careers to passing along their wisdom, that we may all gain.

I wish to honor the many *A Course in Miracles* teachers I have been blessed to come to know as friends, peers, and co-teachers of God. Those with whom I have worked directly include (in alphabetical order) Aaron Abke, Tom and Linda Carpenter, Diane Cirincione, Maria Felipe, David Fishman, Bill Free, KironJ Gardner, Larry Glenn, Jennifer Hadley, David and Svava Hoffmeister, Robert and Hollie Holden, Mark Anthony Lord, Miranda Macpherson, Lisa Natoli, Dr. Robert Rosenthal, Michael Stillwater, Maloah Stillwater, and

Corinne Zupko. There are many more. My apologies if I have overlooked anyone. God knows who you are and the contribution you are making.

Deepest respect for the Foundation for Inner Peace, which has nobly proliferated ACIM since its inception, made it easily and freely accessible online, and expanded its distribution into many foreign languages. Appreciation to current Foundation President Tamara Morgan, and all of the staff and volunteers.

It is my joy and honor to co-create with the Miracle Network, which brings Course teachings to the United Kingdom and worldwide online. Dan Strodl, Teresa Yiannaco, Ian Patrick, Sharon Scarth, and other staff provide a huge service to the British community and beyond.

Special acknowledgment to my friend and brother in Spirit, Nishank Mehta, whom I call "the Johnny Appleseed of India," bringing miracles teachings to the people of that great nation.

As always, I deeply thank all of my readers, who magnify the messages of this book by receiving them, absorbing them, and living them. You make all of my writing worthwhile, and I salute you for your courage and action to call for miracles in your life, and to bless the lives of those you touch.

About the Author

ALAN COHEN, M.A., holds degrees in psychology and human organizational development.

He is the author of 32 popular inspirational books, including the best-selling *A Course in Miracles Made Easy* and the award-winning *A Deep Breath of Life*. He is a contributing writer for the #1 *New York Times* best-selling series *Chicken Soup for the Soul*, and he is featured in the book *101 Top Experts Who Help Us Improve Our Lives*. His books have been translated into 32 foreign languages.

Alan has served on the faculty of Montclair State College, Omega Institute for Holistic Studies, and en*Theos Academy for Optimal Living.

He is a featured presenter in the award-winning documentary *Finding Joe*, celebrating the teachings of Joseph Campbell. His work has been presented on CNN, Oprah.com, and in *USA Today*, *The Washington Post*, and *Huffington Post*. His monthly column *From the Heart* is published in magazines internationally.

Alan is the founder and Director of the Foundation for Holistic Life Coaching. He also keynotes and presents programs on themes of life mastery, spiritual development, and vision psychology.

For information on Alan Cohen's books, seminars,
life coach training, online courses, videos,
and audio recordings, visit:

www.alancohen.com

Facebook:
www.facebook.com/AlanCohenAuthor

YouTube:
@AlanCohenAuthor
www.youtube.com/user/Cowinn327

The Miracle Network

I encourage you to participate in the Miracle Network by subscribing to its online magazine and participating in its webinars, seminars, study groups, and social gatherings. The organization is guided by love and the pure intention to serve. In *A Course in Miracles*, Jesus underscores the importance of minds joining together for healing and mutual upliftment. The Miracle Network nobly serves this purpose. It is my honor to be associated with the fine people who direct it and the many volunteers and program participants. The Miracle Network is a registered U.K. charity (reg. number 1108852) worthy of your donations. A portion of the proceeds from this book is donated to the Miracle Network.

For more information, contact:

Miracle Network

www.miracles.org.uk

info@miracles.org.uk

Telephone +44 (020) 7262 0209

Learn More with Alan Cohen

If you have enjoyed ***Of Course in Miracles***, you may want to deepen your understanding and inspiration by participating in Alan Cohen's in-person seminars, online courses, life coach training, or online subscription programs.

Inspirational Quote for the Day
An uplifting idea e-mailed to you each day (free)

Monthly e-Newsletter
Insightful articles and announcements of upcoming events (free)

Alan's YouTube Channel
Live and recorded presentations
for practical spiritual living (free)

The Coaching Room
One-to-one live online coaching with Alan (free)

Webinars
Interactive programs on topics relevant to spirituality,
self-empowerment, and holistic living

Online Courses
In-depth experiential exploration of healing, relationships, prosperity, prayer, metaphysics, and stress management

Life Coach Training
Become a certified professional holistic life coach or enhance your career and personal life with coaching skills

A Course in Miracles
Ongoing study group and retreat to empower you to master the principles and skills of this life-changing program

For information about all of these offerings, and more, visit
www.alancohen.com

Made in United States
North Haven, CT
16 July 2024

54849607R00134